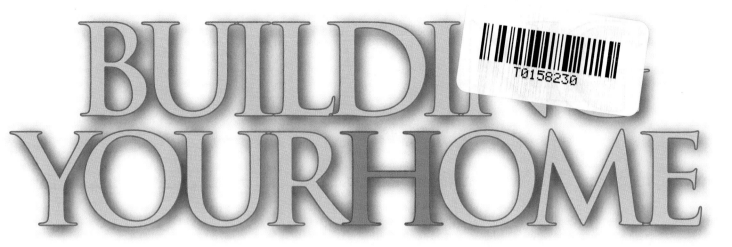

BUILDING YOURHOME

AN INSIDER'S GUIDE
SECOND EDITION

CAROL SMITH

BuilderBooks.com

A Service of
NAHB
NATIONAL ASSOCIATION
OF HOME BUILDERS

Building Your Home: An Insider's Guide, Second Edition, by Carol Smith

Christine B. Charlip   Publisher, BuilderBooks
Doris M. Tennyson   Senior Editor
Torrie Singletary   Assistant Editor
Granville Woodson   Cover Design
Circle Graphics   Composition
Transcontinental   Printing

Gerald M. Howard   NAHB Executive Vice President and CEO
Mark Pursell   NAHB Senior Staff Vice President, Marketing & Sales Group
Lakisha Campbell   NAHB Staff Vice President, Publications & Affinity Programs

This publication is designed to provide accurate and authoritative information in regard to the subject matter covered. It is sold with the understanding that the publisher is not engaged in rendering legal, accounting, or other professional service. If legal advice or other expert assistance is required, the services of a competent professional should be sought.

—From a Declaration of Principles jointly adopted by a Committee of the American Bar Association and a Committee of Publishers and Associations.

Library of Congress Cataloging-in-Publication Data

Smith, Carol, 1946-
  Building your home : an insider's guide / Carol Smith.
    p. cm.
  Previously published as: Building your home. 2001.
  Includes bibliographical references.
  ISBN 0-86718-604-6
  1. House construction—Popular works. I. Building your home. II. Title.
  TH4815.B86 2005
  690'.837—dc22
                                2005013432

For further information, please contact:

BuilderBooks.com

National Association of Home Builders
1201 15th Street, NW
Washington, DC 20005-2800
800-223-2665
Visit us online at www.BuilderBooks.com

Contents

Figures

Chapter 7 Preliminary Steps

Chapter 8 Construction Process

Chapter 9 Construction Sequence

Chapter 10 Home Owner Orientation

Chapter 11 Closing

Chapter 12 Moving In

Chapter 13 Your Home Care Plan

Chapter 14 Warranty Service

About the Author

Internationally renowned, Carol Smith is a customer relations expert with 30 years of experience in the home building, customer relations, real estate, and mortgage industries with home owners and builders alike. A bestselling author of nearly a dozen books focusing on home building, Carol's successful books include *Customer Service for Home Builders*; *Warranty Service for Home Builders*; *Meetings with Clients*; *Homeowner Manual, 2nd ed.*; *Dear Homeowner: A Book of Customer Service Letters*; and other products. She founded the Association for Customer Relations Professionals and speaks to standing room only audiences at the International Builders' Show of the National Association of Home Builders, at state and local builders' association functions, and at meetings in Canada, Australia, and other countries. To read her bimonthly newsletter *Home Address*, go to www.csmithhomeaddress.com, click on *Resources* and *Home Address* newsletter.

She has been married to a custom builder for nearly 17 tempestuous, exciting, wonderful years—most of them spent remodeling their home.

Acknowledgments

Second Edition

Special thanks to David Crump, NAHB Director of Legal Research, for his assistance regarding such topics as mechanic's liens, mold, contracts, disclaimers, and other issues; George Middleton, NAHB Senior Manager of Labor, Safety, and Health; Lawrence Brown, CBO, NAHB Construction Codes and Standards Specialist; and Daniel Blum, Building Inspector, Washington, D.C. Thanks also to Gretchen Hesbacher of the International Code Council (a membership association—to learn more, visit www.iccsafe.org).

First Edition

The author would like to thank the many people who reviewed the outline and/or manuscript and provided excellent suggestions on ways to improve the book: John and Kathie Ball, Louisville, Colorado; Brad Bradley, Bradley Design, Hutchinson, Kansas; Sam Bradley, Sam Bradley Homes, Springfield, Missouri; Thomas E. Denny, Pioneer Bank of Longmont, Longmont, Colorado; Mary DeCrescenzo, NAHB Legal Services; John N. Drake, Drake Homes, St. Charles, Missouri; David Handy, Castle Rock, Colorado; Robert Hankin, Compass Homes, Inc., Highland Mills, New York; Stephen D. Hannan, Howard County Office of Consumer Homes, Inc., Columbia, Maryland; John Howard, The John Howard Companies, Mobile, Alabama; Mike Humphrey, David Weekley Homes, Houston, Texas; Carol Hyman, NAHB Builder Business Services; David Jaffe, NAHB Legal Services; Andrew H. Johnson, Colorado Mortgage Professionals, Englewood, Colorado; Zoe LaGassa, NAHB Public Affairs; Joseph Laquatra, Department of Design and Environmental Analysis, Cornell University, Ithaca, New York; Bruce and Kathy Leary, Arapahoe Custom Homes, Inc., Aurora, Colorado; Hazel McColley, Parker, Colorado; Linda McGhee, NAHB Financial Institutions and Production Finance; Valena Mulhern, National Title, Denver, Colorado; John J. Piazza, Sr., Piazza Construction, Inc., Mount Vernon, Washington; Kim Post, Newell Construction, Inc., Caledonia, Michigan; Jon Radcliff, Ashlyn Creek, LLC, Littleton, Colorado; George Rose, Montgomery County Office of Consumer Affairs (Housing); Rockville, Maryland; Ryan and Donna Schlaefer, Aurora, Colorado; and William Young, NAHB Consumer Affairs.

Disclaimer

The sample contracts and clauses shown in this book are provided for educational purposes in order to illustrate the principles discussed. They should not be used as forms. These contracts are designed to cover the major topics of consideration for most new residential construction contracts. However, the contract provisions shown do not and cannot apply to every situation, nor do they comply with any particular state law. Some of the provisions will not apply to a particular situation, while in other cases additional terms may be appropriate. Laws can vary, and some states may require specific language and formats for certain contracts. New home buyers should work with their builders and attorneys to prepare documents that meet their particular needs.

Introduction

With so many books available for people wanting to have a home built, why write another? Because the books on the shelves leave some things unsaid. I travel all over this country and abroad, providing training programs for home builders. My main focus is customer satisfaction: philosophy, objectives, systems, and staff skills. I've interviewed thousands of home owners who've described varying levels of satisfaction.

For years I've watched home builders and their buyers struggle through unnecessary misunderstandings and conflicting interpretations. I've seen builders with the best of intentions make mistakes because they habitually fail to see things from their customer's point of view. I've encountered a few builders more concerned with profit than integrity who made enemies for the entire home building profession. I have also seen buyers manipulate what builders tell them to get more than their fair share, using customer satisfaction as a tool rather than a mutual goal. Still other buyers end up dissatisfied because they did not look, read, or listen carefully enough. Most often, the problems I observed arose because good people buying new homes were upset with good people building new homes, all because the two groups did not communicate clearly, or enough.

This book brings you an industry insider's perspective on what buyers should expect, what questions they should ask, and who is responsible for what tasks. My objective: to help home buyers become informed customers who understand the building process and the product they are buying. With a realistic perspective, buyers are more likely to succeed in matching their vision of that ideal home with the site, design, builder, and budget that comes closest to creating that home.

Builders and home buyers in our country use many ways to finance, build, deliver, and close a new home. Builders in the area where you want to live may do things a bit differently from what you are familiar with or from what is presented here. I'll discuss typical methods, forms, and steps in the process. You should expect regional variations and additions. But one thing remains the same wherever you are: the process begins when you decide you want to build a new home.

The Decision to Build 1

Some say the decision to build a home starts when you select a location. Others suggest that the process begins with an appealing floor plan. For many, money is the common motivator. Quite simply, the decision to build a new home begins when you become dissatisfied with your current home. Too big, too small, too near, too far, too plain, too old. No place to park the cars. Not enough room for the kids to play (or sleep). Not enough windows. Too much yard. Rent is not tax-deductible. Perhaps your current home is five states from the new job—or the new grandchild.

Reasons to Move

Consider your reasons for moving. What do you intend to accomplish by having a home built? Being involved from the beginning in the construction of your new home provides a unique sense of ownership. Not only will the home you build be new, it also will reflect your personal tastes. This home will belong to you and your family in a special way.

What do you expect to have in a new home that you do not have now? What features and characteristics do you want to duplicate? Equally important, what things do you want to avoid? As you begin to consider such questions, you have begun the exciting process of building a new home.

Selecting a resale home might satisfy many of your reasons for moving. Yet over a million families purchase a newly built home each year. The home building experience appeals to many of us. Some families select new homes that are ready to move into; others begin with a blank sheet of paper and become intimately involved in every step of design and construction. Most home buyers fall somewhere between the two. And all share the anticipation, excitement, and work of moving into a new home.

"I Know What I Like"

In terms of the product and the process, you have more choices than ever before. Each affects many others—physically, financially, or both. Along with the practical choices, a new home involves subjective elements; details of your home reflect your values and taste. You need information and introspection to arrive at decisions that meet your requirements while you stay within your budget.

Selecting or developing a design that will serve your family now and for years to come requires an analysis of your current lifestyle and anticipation of your future needs. Whether you work from existing plans or a blank sheet of paper, coordinating decisions about size, shape, traffic flow, and finish materials can seem overwhelming. Next, how can you tell if your home is well built? Value and quality are especially complicated issues when the product is a new home.

The experience of building a home is complicated, exciting, scary, fun, expensive, gratifying, time-consuming, and wonderful—sometimes all in the same day.

One of the most complex handcrafted products available in our world, a home contains tens of thousands of parts, assembled by dozens of people. The most accomplished production builder does not produce two alike. Design, selection, and quality issues arise in every home. Some opinions on these issues come from factual knowledge; others involve subjective views that come from years of experience. Opinions differ with the knowledge and experience of each architect, designer, builder, real estate agent, and home buyer. Fairly judging the final product requires an understanding of the properties of the materials, methods of installation, and the way all the parts interact.

Knowledge

Your knowledge of new home construction expands as you listen, read, and observe; lack of understanding can lead to disappointment. Like all professions, the home building industry has its own jargon. If you familiarize yourself with its terminology, you'll find asking questions and evaluating answers easier. No matter how much you think you know about new home construction now, you'll find you know much more by the time you move into your newly built home. Fortunately, you don't need to become an expert in every aspect of home construction. Many professionals are available to help you reach your home building goals. At times you may defer to these professionals' judgment.

Investment

Your home is usually your family's biggest investment and often its best. Not only does a home provide a place to live for many years, it can provide equity in later years. The equity Americans have in their homes accounts for more than half the total net worth of the typical home owning family.

The financial arrangements you make at the time of purchase affect the long-term value of your investment as well as your monthly budget. The lending profession is constantly restructuring its products to fit a variety of customer situations. Thirty-year, fifteen-year, and adjustable rate mortgages are just the beginning. Each loan program offers advantages and disadvantages, depending on your financial goals. You'll also want to keep in mind the tax implications of these financial arrangements.

Time and Emotion

Building a new home puts significant demands on your time. Meetings consume much of that time. Many of these meetings will occur during normal business hours, Monday

Regardless of how many meetings you expect, plan on more. However many decisions you expect, expect more.

through Friday. Home buyers clearly expect to be kept informed along the way, and they want opportunities to be involved and to ask questions. Builders have responded by offering routine scheduled meetings. While these meetings are extremely helpful to buyers, staffing limitations and other practical details often prevent holding them in the evenings or on weekends.

However much worry and fun you think the process will bring, get ready for more of both. Many compare the building process to a roller coaster ride, a series of highs and lows. For instance, when you stand in your newly framed family room deciding where to put the sofa, the loan application paperwork seems less annoying than when you filled it out.

Applying Logic to Dreams

The actual construction of your home follows a logical sequence. The planning that leads to building could be logical, but it's rarely that simple. A common question is which do you find

Reprinted with permission from Advanced Custom Home, Inc., Hilton Head Island, South Carolina.

first: the lot, the builder, a real estate agent, a lender, or an architect? The answer is yes. You can build a home with any and all of these choices as the starting point. Whether you decide to work with a production, semi-custom, or custom builder, the process of building involves many subjects: budget, builder, budget, location, budget, floor plan, budget, elevation (exterior views of a home), budget (Figure 1.1).

In what order do you make these decisions? Springfield, Missouri, custom builder Sam Bradley correctly observes, "You do a little of all of it at once." Some buyers consider the decision for years before they build a home; others take shortcuts that can result in problems. Bradley advises prospects to take their time. "Prospective clients come to me with nightmares—blueprints that don't fit on the lot they've purchased. In that case, do you throw away the lot or the blueprints?"

Logic suggests that you establish your budget before making design

Figure 1.1
Will an Elegant Stairway Fit into Your Budget?

decisions. But no one has found a way to keep visions of the front elevation from flashing through your mind as you discuss mortgage rates. The tangle of memories, current needs, schedules, and costs means that you make few of your new home decisions in isolation or in a predictable sequence (Figure 1.2). Washington, D.C., area home buyer Zoe LaGassa described it well: "You may be looking at a site but thinking about how you always wanted a red sink in your kitchen."

Building a home is an once-in-a-lifetime experience for many customers. Finding a comfortable balance among quality, features, and price is a tremendous challenge. Your efforts should result in a home you enjoy and in which you take pride. Ultimately, when you finish unpacking, we hope that you look at your new home, think over the home-building experience, and conclude, "Building this house was the best thing we ever did."

**Figure 1.2
Do You Want a
Balcony for Your
Bedroom?**

Financing

"How Am I Going to Pay for This House?"

2

John and Mary's home was completed under budget and ahead of schedule. They selected new furniture with the savings. A carpet sale allowed them to order the highest grade carpet at the cost of standard grade. This savings paid for their kitchen appliance upgrades. Big Muscle Moving agreed to move them at a reduced cost since it had a truck in the area. As a welcome gift, New City Gas & Electric contributed 90 days of free service. Green Bucks Mortgage lowered its interest rate because its loan quota for the month had been met. Because John and Mary were so pleasant to work with, their builder waived any profit. The closing coordinator called to say the settlement figures had changed again. Once more the cash John needed for closing was reduced, this time by $875. One more phone call, John thought with a grin, and they'll give us money at closing. He decided to write letters of appreciation just as the buzz of the alarm clock jolted him awake. . . .

J ohn's dream sequence is so out of touch you may wonder if a mere alarm clock is sufficient to return him to reality. For most people a home represents the biggest financial and physical purchase they ever make. Predicting the exact cost is at best a guess until all your choices are finalized. Even then, unexpected circumstances such as poor weather, a large rock on the site, or falling in love with a hand-painted tile can affect the most meticulous budget. Information, planning, and self-discipline offer your best assurance of keeping costs under control. As you begin to think about your new home, think about how you are going to pay for it. By considering finances from the beginning and as part of every decision, you make smarter choices and avoid disappointments.

Your Assets

Survey your financial assets by listing available cash such as checking and savings accounts or CDs near maturity. Will additional cash accumulate during construction of your home—a salary increase, bonus, profit-sharing distribution, tax refund, or other reliable source? The cash you have on hand or readily available is referred to as your liquidity. Some liquidity is essential at the beginning stages, through the building process, and after completion of the new home. You are likely to need cash for loan application fees, the down payment, closing fees, move-in costs, and settling expenses such as landscaping and window coverings (or at least sheets and push pins).

Next consider assets you can turn into cash. The classic example is the equity in a home you already own. Equity is the amount that would remain after subtracting the present mortgage balance and the sale expenses from the price you get when you sell the home. Other assets might include a cash gift from a family member, an inheritance, maturing bonds, or the cash value of an insurance policy. This time might be just right for you to auction off that Van Gogh you picked up for $15 at a garage sale.

Another potential asset is sweat equity—construction work you perform yourself. If you enjoy cabinet building and are highly skilled at it, you may want to build and install the ones for your new home. Have the value of this labor credited to you or use your skills to reduce the price of the home. However, sweat equity agreements are not without risks, and many builders prefer not to use them. If interested, ask potential builders about their policy on these types of agreements early and document any such agreements in the contract.

Finding a Lender

When people need to borrow money, many of them think first of their banks. When the money is for a home, mortgage companies come to mind next. Both are possibilities, but explore all options, including savings and loan associations, commercial banks, credit unions, and mortgage brokers. Most states have housing finance agencies that work with low- and moderate-income households. Insurance companies and even department stores are getting into the mortgage-lending business. The builder or real estate agent you work with may have suggestions on obtaining financing.

Prequalifying

Ask one or more potential lenders to prequalify you for your home purchase. Prequalifying means your financial position has been informally reviewed to determine how much money you can borrow. It provides several benefits:

- No matter what type of home you seek, prequalifying provides you with critical planning information. By knowing your budget from the beginning, you can avoid time-consuming and disappointing cutbacks in your new home plans.
- If you begin with buying land for a home, prequalification figures can help you make the right choice. Buying a lot can alter your cash position and therefore your house budget. Without some preliminary guidance, you could end up with a lot but not enough financial leverage to build on it.
- Prequalifying can identify details in your financial picture that might interfere with your plans. Discovering them early prevents a mad scramble through dusty boxes of financial records two days before closing and leaves time for more mundane tasks—such as packing.
- As part of your prequalifying activities, carefully review your credit report. You may find some errors. I once discovered our credit report included a $6,500 loan from a bank we never heard of in a city where we'd never lived. If your credit report includes inaccurate information, the sooner you begin correcting it the better. (For more information on this topic, see Figure 2.1.)

Figure 2.1 Establishing Credit

Order a Copy of Your Credit Report

Credit reporting agencies are listed in your local telephone directory under "credit." Your credit report will include the following:

- Your current name, previous names under which you had credit
- Your current and previous residences
- Where you work and have worked, often with salary
- Judgments, public records such as lawsuits, divorce, child support litigation
- Information supplied by your creditors

  —amount they loaned you
  —your record of repayment
  —your current balance
  —your current monthly obligation

Correct Errors

The Fair Credit Reporting Act of 1971 protects consumers against errors on credit reports. If you discover an error on your credit history, notify the credit agency in writing. The law obligates it to reinvestigate. If an inaccuracy is confirmed, the credit agency must change your report. If the data is accurate, you can add your version of the dispute to the file. Accurate negative information can remain on your credit history for a maximum of 7 years and bankruptcy for 10 years.

Establish Credit

Establishing credit is a rite of passage that can be frustrating. These hints may make it easier:

- Establish your residence and stay put.
- Get a job and stay put, or at least stay in the same line of work.
- Borrow a small amount from a bank, credit union, or department store and pay it back exactly on time or even a bit early.
- Be patient. Time alone can solve some of the obstacles to credit.
- Consider the possibility of having a cosigner. Usually a relative or friend, this borrower guarantees to pay if you do not.
- When you get credit, use it wisely; poor reports and serious problems can haunt you for years.

Benefit from the Equal Credit Opportunity

When you apply for a mortgage, the Federal Equal Credit Opportunity Act protects you from discrimination based on race, color, religion, national origin, sex, marital status, or age. It doesn't guarantee you a mortgage loan, but lenders cannot deny your application because of these factors. If you have questions about a credit agency, contact the Federal Trade Commission, Division of Credit Practices, 600 Pennsylvania Avenue, N.W., Washington, DC 20580, 202-326-2222 (to connect with frequently called offices), and 202-326-2000 (for specific staff members), http://www.ftc.gov/. You also can call the Federal Deposit Insurance Corporation at 877-ASKFDIC (877-275-3342) or for TDD at 800-925-4618, between 8 a.m. and 8 p.m. Monday through Friday, Eastern Standard Time, or go to http://www.fdic.gov/.

Prequalifying does not obligate you to do business with a particular institution. Neither does it commit the lender to granting the loan you request.

Do not confuse prequalifying with preapproval, which requires formal application and complete processing. Prequalifying does not obligate you to do business with a particular institution. Neither does it commit the lender to granting the loan you request. Nearly all lenders will happily prequalify you.

Remember, the answers lenders give you are only as accurate as the information you provide them. Be prepared to describe your assets, employment, income, and liabilities. This information is fed into a computer, which calculates your borrowing power by comparing the data to the requirements of various loan programs. In a few minutes it identifies the loan programs that fit your circumstances. The benefits do not end there, however.

Comparing Lenders and Programs

When you visit lenders for prequalification, collect information about loan programs for comparison purposes. Ask for a list of items required to formalize your application. An ideal lender makes you feel appreciated and comfortable and offers a loan program that suits your needs. The lender's staff should be accessible and responsive. Comparing costs is important, but so are the tone and style of the lender's communications. When evaluating costs, look beyond lender fees and interest rates. Consider down payment requirements and which closing costs you will pay when the home is complete.

Down Payment

The *down payment* is the difference between the price of the home and the amount of your permanent loan. The earnest money deposit you give the builder when you sign the contract is part of the down payment. If you're building a home on a lot you own, your lender may consider the value of your land as part of the down payment. Options, upgrades, and changes you pay for during construction can also count toward the down payment total. You pay the balance of the down payment at closing. Figure 2.2 offers a worksheet for determining your available down payment.

Closing Costs

New home closing costs are the charges and fees associated with transferring ownership of real estate. Often they are estimated at 5 percent of the loan amount, but they can vary. Chapter 11 provides a detailed discussion of closing costs. Keep in mind that the higher your closing costs run, the less cash you'll have for the down payment and other items such as new home options. The financial aspect of building a home parallels the design aspect: changing one detail changes others.

Amount You Can Borrow

Prequalifying may indicate you can borrow more than you thought, a pleasant if uncommon surprise. Remember, the lender arrived at that figure based on the circumstances you described. A change in salary, marital status, a big win in the lottery, or a new car loan will change those circumstances and affect the loan amount.

Figure 2.2 Down Payment Worksheet

Available Funds

Equity in present home $ _____

Savings, savings certificates   _____

Investments   _____

Insurance (cash value)   _____

Other funds (such as a cash gift)   _____

Total available funds   _____

Minus amount you want to keep in savings   _____

Adjusted Total Available Funds   _____

Expected Expenses

Settlement costs (estimate 5 percent of loan amount)   _____

Moving costs   _____

Landscaping   _____

Other expected expenses   _____

Total Expected Expenses   _____

Down Payment

Adjusted total available funds   _____

Minus total expected expenses   _____

Amount Available for Down Payment   _____

If you qualify for less than you had hoped, find out what changes—such as paying off a debt—might qualify you for a larger loan. Variable- (adjustable-) rate loans are often approved for higher amounts or carry more lenient qualification requirements because of their lower initial payments. If you expect to receive a substantial amount of income during construction, you may opt for a smaller loan and pay cash for some items during construction.

Another solution is to identify items that you could omit from the original construction and add in the future. For example, postponing a deck or covered patio might make the numbers work. Your builder or design team can help you identify such items. Before you alter your plans, though, talk to another lender. Lender programs and requirements vary.

Permanent Financing: Your Mortgage

Believe it or not, getting a mortgage has its advantages. Qualifying for a mortgage enables you to buy more house than you might afford with cash on hand. Called leveraging, this concept facilitates much of the activity that goes on in the business world, as well as in home sales. Mortgage interest costs are usually tax-deductible. Points paid at closing are considered mortgage interest and as such are deductible in most cases. Always check your specific rights and responsibilities by reviewing the Internal Revenue Service's latest "simplified" paperwork or talk to your tax accountant.

The disadvantages of mortgages are equally well known. Completing all those forms takes time. You always need some document that you cannot find, most likely because it's in a shoe box with the 1981 summer vacation pictures. Mortgage applicants typically feel as if their privacy is being invaded. "Why do they care if great-grandmother Gertie made her fortune running rum," you grumble. "A gift is a gift." You'll feel less invaded if you consider the lender's point of view: what would you want to know about a person to whom you were lending this amount of money?

Mortgages come in many shapes and sizes. Fixed-rate, adjustable-rate, graduated, balloon, biweekly, jumbos, buy-down, Federal Housing Administration (FHA), the Veterans Administration (VA), growing equity mortgage (GEM), graduated payment mortgage (GPM)—the list goes on. Each program has unique traits. Lenders must make complete disclosure of all the terms and conditions that apply to home loans. Matching a loan program to your circumstances requires detailed knowledge. Understanding common loan elements helps you sort through the possibilities.

Interest Amortization

All mortgages have one thing in common—an interest rate, the rate you are charged for the amount of money, or principal, you borrow. The principal and interest total is amortized over the length of your mortgage. In other words, in the early years most of your monthly payment goes toward interest; a small amount goes toward the actual loan. As years pass that gradually reverses until, near the end, most of your payment applies to the principal.

Fixed-Rate Mortgage

With a fixed-rate mortgage the interest rate stays the same through the term of the loan. The 30-year, fixed-rate mortgage remains popular because of its stability. A 15-year, fixed-rate mortgage pays off the loan sooner and accumulates equity faster, meaning the payment is higher and therefore more difficult to qualify for. Fixed-rate mortgages appeal to home buyers who expect to remain in their homes many years and to those who prefer predictability.

Adjustable- or Variable-Rate Mortgage

Adjustable-rate mortgages (ARMs) have changeable interest rates. ARMs are usually easier to qualify for because their initial lower interest rate results in a lower payment, at least in the beginning years.

The rate is tied to a financial index such as six-month Treasury bills. If the index goes up or down, so does the mortgage rate—and your payment. Typically, the lender can adjust the rate once a year. Rate caps limit how much the rate changes and some programs include an option to convert the loan to a fixed-rate mortgage in the future (for a fee). Adjustable mortgages appeal to buyers who expect to stay in their homes for just a few years or those whose income will steadily increase in the future.

Origination Fee

Lenders charge an origination fee, typically 1 percent of the loan amount. This fee pays the lender for the services of the loan executive and other staff who work on your loan file.

Discount Points or "Points"

If someone gave a prize for the most aggravating aspect of mortgages, it would probably go to discount points, a one-time charge sometimes levied by the lender. The discount applies to the interest rate you pay on your mortgage. You receive this discount because you pay some of the interest in a lump sum at the closing table. Each point is 1 percent of the loan amount. On a $200,000 loan, a point would equal $2,000. Each point you pay reduces the interest rate on a 30-year, fixed-rate loan 1/8 of a percentage point. The points you pay are usually tax-deductible as mortgage interest in the year you pay them.

Principal, Interest, Taxes, and Insurance

Mortgage payments are usually made up of principal, interest, taxes, and insurance (PITI). The principal and interest are calculated based on loan amount, interest rate, and term of the loan. Taxes in this context refer to local property taxes. The (hazard) insurance and usually covers theft, fire, wind, hail, and other catastrophic damage to the structure.

Ratios

Lenders consider three ratios during mortgage processing. The first is the housing expense ratio, also called the front-end ratio. To arrive at this ratio, divide your gross (before tax) monthly income by the proposed monthly mortgage payment. If your monthly income is $4,000 and the proposed monthly mortgage payment is $1,000, you have a front-end or housing expense ratio of 25 percent. Twenty-eight percent is a typical limit for the housing expense ratio. (VA loans do not consider this ratio.)

To arrive at the second ratio—the debt or back-end ratio—add your long-term payments, including mortgage, car, furniture, student loans, child support, charge card debt, and so on. Divide this total by your gross monthly income. Lenders typically use a limit of 36 percent. VA loans, however, use a debt ratio of 41 percent as the guideline.

Compensating factors, such as a large savings balance, can affect these guidelines. Selecting an energy-efficient home could qualify you for more generous ratios from your lender. Lower utility bills, the thinking goes, leave you with more money to pay your mortgage.

The third ratio considered in mortgage processing is called the loan-to-value ratio. If the home appraises for $100,000 and the loan program allows up to an 80 percent loan-to-value, a qualified borrower can obtain an $80,000 mortgage. The buyer pays the remaining 20 percent as the down payment.

FHA-Insured Loans

The Federal Housing Administration does not lend money, but it does insure mortgage loans. Some FHA programs require as little as 3 to 5 percent down. With an FHA mortgage you'll pay a premium for the insurance, which you can add to the loan and spread over the life of the mortgage.

VA-Guaranteed Loans

Qualifying veterans of military service are eligible for Veteran Administration loans. These VA loans are not insured but are guaranteed from 25 to 50 percent of appraised value. Lenders usually believe the home could sell for at least 75 percent of appraised value in the event of a default. The VA guarantee of the other 25 percent covers any balance, thereby protecting the lender from loss. Therefore a veteran can sometimes qualify for a mortgage without any down payment.

Conventional Loans

Conventional loans are neither FHA insured nor VA guaranteed. Although most conventional lenders prefer a down payment of at least 20 percent, many programs require as little as 5 percent down. Since neither the FHA nor the VA assure these loans, borrowers who put down less than 20 percent must purchase private mortgage insurance.

Private Mortgage Insurance

In the event of foreclosure, the lender sells the home. Private mortgage insurance (PMI) pays the difference between the loan balance and the selling price and thus protects the lender's interest. The private mortgage insurance company reviews the applicant's credit history and other factors just as the lender does. If approved, charges for processing the application and the premium show up as a closing expense. If the applicant is not approved, options include making a larger down payment to avoid the requirement altogether or submitting the file to another private mortgage insurance company that may use different qualifying criteria.

Loan Application

Prepare for your loan application appointment by collecting the required documents and information. Figure 2.3 lists items commonly needed. Expect the application process to take more than an hour, and you need to be prepared to sign many forms and disclosures. You should receive a copy of every document you sign. Read everything and ask questions. Do not hesitate to mention concerns that you have regarding your assets, income, or credit

---

Figure 2.3 Mortgage Application Checklist

Contract

☐ Legal description of the property
☐ Price

Personal Information

☐ Social Security number and driver's license for all borrowers
☐ Home addresses for the last 2 years
☐ Divorce decree and separation agreement, if applicable

Income

☐ Most recent pay stubs
☐ Documentation on any supplemental income: bonuses, commissions
☐ Names, addresses, and phone numbers of all employers for last 2 years
☐ W-2s for last 2 years
☐ If self-employed or commissioned sales, copies of last 2 years' tax returns with all schedules and year-to-date profit and loss for current year, signed by an accountant
☐ Documentation of alimony or child support, if such income is to be considered for the loan
☐ Latest statement from stock and/or bond investment account

Real Estate Owned

☐ Names, addresses, phone numbers, and account numbers of all mortgage lenders and landlords for the last 7 years
☐ Copies of leases and 2 years' tax returns for any rental property
☐ Market value estimate

Liquid Assets

☐ Complete names, addresses, phone numbers, and account numbers for all bank accounts (including investment accounts)
☐ Copies of last 3 months' statements for all bank accounts
☐ Copies of any notes receivable
☐ Value of other assets (auto, households goods, and collectibles)
☐ Cash value of life insurance policies
☐ Vested interest in retirement funds, IRAs, Keoghs, 401-Ks

Liabilities

☐ Name and account number for all revolving charge cards, balance, and current monthly payment amount
☐ Name, addresses, phone numbers, and account numbers for all installment debt; approximate balance and monthly payment
☐ Alimony or child support payments
☐ Names, addresses, phone numbers, and account numbers of accounts recently paid off, if used to establish credit

history (Figure 2.4). This time is not for shyness. The lender's job is to understand your particular financial circumstances. Expect to pay for a credit report and an appraisal when you submit the application.

Good Faith Estimate

The Good Faith Estimate, shown in Figure 2.5 lists the costs you will incur at the closing on your new home. The key word here is estimate. Some of the figures change based on which day of the month the closing occurs. See Chapter 11 for more details.

Truth-in-Lending Disclosure

The Truth-in-Lending Disclosure shows the cost of your specific financing as a percentage and as a dollar amount. You can see an example in Figure 2.6. An important detail shows whether prepayment penalties apply. The Truth-in-Lending Disclosure lists the charge for a late payment, usually calculated as a percentage of the payment; 5 percent is common.

Credit Report and Verifications

Your lender obtains your credit report at the time of application. If more than 30 days pass between the initial credit report and the closing, the lender may update the report just

**Figure 2.4
The Goal of a
Mortgage
Application:
A New Home**

These four-story, custom townhouses overlook the Intercoastal Waterway and Windmill Harbour, Hilton Head Island, South Carolina, and feature distinctive floor plans and special amenities.

Reprinted with permission from Advanced Custom Home, Inc., Hilton Head Island, South Carolina.

**Figure 2.5
Good Faith
Estimate**

GOOD FAITH ESTIMATE

Applicants:
Property Addr: 5036 Perth Court,
Prepared By: Cherrywood Home Loans Ph. 303-486-8900
18607 E 48th Avenue Suite 110, Denver, CO 80249

Application No: 050304006
Date Prepared: 03/04/2005
Loan Program: 30 Yr Fixed

The information provided below reflects estimates of the charges which you are likely to incur at the settlement of your loan. The fees listed are estimates-actual charges may be more or less. Your transaction may not involve a fee for every item listed. The numbers listed beside the estimates generally correspond to the numbered lines contained in the HUD-1 settlement statement which you will be receiving at settlement. The HUD-1 settlement statement will show you the actual cost for items paid at settlement.

Total Loan Amount $ 160,000   Interest Rate: 5.750 %   Term: 360 / 360 mths

800	ITEMS PAYABLE IN CONNECTION WITH LOAN:			PFC S F POC
801	Loan Origination Fee	1.000%	$	1,600.00 √
802	Loan Discount			
803	Appraisal Fee			325.00
804	Credit Report			23.00
805	Lender's Inspection Fee			
808	Mortgage Broker Fee			
809	Tax Related Service Fee			
810	Processing Fee			450.00 √
811	Underwriting Fee			
812	Wire Transfer Fee			
	Investor Administrative Fee			475.00 √
	Flood Certificate			15.00 √
	Final Inspection			75.00 √

1100	TITLE CHARGES:			PFC S F POC
1101	Closing or Escrow Fee:	Town & Country Title	$	200.00 √
1105	Document Preparation Fee			
1106	Notary Fees			
1107	Attorney Fees			
1108	Title Insurance:	Town & Country Title		350.00
	Courier Fee			25.00 √
	Real Estate Closing Fee -Town & Country Title			75.00 √

1200	GOVERNMENT RECORDING & TRANSFER CHARGES:			PFC S F POC
1201	Recording Fees:		$	120.00
1202	City/County Tax/Stamps:			
1203	State Tax/Stamps:			25.00

1300	ADDITIONAL SETTLEMENT CHARGES:			PFC S F POC
1302	Pest Inspection		$	

packages at the Design Center).

		Estimated Closing Costs		3,758.00

900	ITEMS REQUIRED BY LENDER TO BE PAID IN ADVANCE:				PFC S F POC
901	Interest for	15 days @ $	25.5556	per day	$	383.33 √
902	Mortgage Insurance Premium				√
903	Hazard Insurance Premium				840.00
904					
905	VA Funding Fee				

1000	RESERVES DEPOSITED WITH LENDER:				PFC S F POC
1001	Hazard Insurance Premium	3 months @ $	70.00 per month	$	210.00
1002	Mortgage Ins. Premium Reserves	months @ $	per month		√
1003	School Tax	months @ $	per month		
1004	Taxes and Assessment Reserves	3 months @ $	125.00 per month		375.00
1005	Flood Insurance Reserves	months @ $	per month		
		months @ $	per month		
		months @ $	per month		
	Aggregate Adjustment				

	Estimated Prepaid Items/Reserves	1,808.33
TOTAL ESTIMATED SETTLEMENT CHARGES		5,566.33

COMPENSATION TO BROKER (Not Paid Out of Loan Proceeds):

YSP 0% - 4%	$	POC

TOTAL ESTIMATED FUNDS NEEDED TO CLOSE:			TOTAL ESTIMATED MONTHLY PAYMENT:	
Purchase Price/Payoff (+)	200,000.00	New First Mortgage(-)	Principal & Interest	933.72
Loan Amount (-)	160,000.00	Sub Financing(-)	Other Financing (P & I)	560.40
Est. Closing Costs (+)	3,758.00	New 2nd Mtg Closing Costs(+) 450.00	Hazard Insurance	70.00
Est. Prepaid Items/Reserves (+)	1,808.33		Real Estate Taxes	125.00
Amount Paid by Seller (-)	1,000.00		Mortgage Insurance	
Second Mortgage	-30,000.00		Homeowner Assn. Dues	
			Other	

Total Est. Funds needed to close		15,016.33	Total Monthly Payment	1,689.12

☐ This Good Faith Estimate is being provided by _____, a mortgage broker, and no lender has been obtained. These estimates are provided pursuant to the Real Estate Settlement Procedures Act of 1974, as amended (RESPA). Additional information can be found in the HUD Special Information Booklet, which is to be provided to you by your mortgage broker or lender, if your application is to purchase residential real property and the lender will take a first lien on the property. The undersigned acknowledges receipt of the booklet "Settlement Costs." and if applicable the Consumer Handbook on ARM Mortgages.

Applicant _____ Date _____ Applicant _____ Date _____

Calyx Form gfe.frm 11/01

Reprinted with permission from Cherrywood Home Loans, LLC, Denver, Colorado.

**Figure 2.6
Truth-in-Lending
Disclosure
Statement**

TRUTH-IN-LENDING DISCLOSURE STATEMENT
(THIS IS NEITHER A CONTRACT NOR A COMMITMENT TO LEND)

Applicants:

Property Address:

Application No:

Prepared By: **Cherrywood Home Loans**
18607 E 48th Avenue Suite 110
Denver , CO 80249
303-486-8900

Date Prepared: **03/04/2005**

ANNUAL PERCENTAGE RATE	FINANCE CHARGE	AMOUNT FINANCED	TOTAL OF PAYMENTS
The cost of your credit as a yearly rate	The dollar amount the credit will cost you	The amount of credit provided to you or on your behalf	The amount you will have paid after making all payments as scheduled
5.920 %	$ 179,434.31	$ 156,701.67	$ 336,135.98

☐ REQUIRED DEPOSIT: The annual percentage rate does not take into account your required deposit
PAYMENTS: Your payment schedule will be:

Number of Payments	Amount of Payments **	When Payments Are Due	Number of Payments	Amount of Payments **	When Payments Are Due	Number of Payments	Amount of Payments **	When Payments Are Due
		Monthly Beginning:			Monthly Beginning:			Monthly Beginning:
359	933.72	07/01/2005						
1	930.50	06/01/2035						

☐ DEMAND FEATURE: This obligation has a demand feature.
☐ VARIABLE RATE FEATURE: This loan contains a variable rate feature. A variable rate disclosure has been provided earlier.

CREDIT LIFE/CREDIT DISABILITY: Credit life insurance and credit disability insurance are not required to obtain credit, and will not be provided unless you sign and agree to pay the additional cost.

Type	Premium	Signature	
Credit Life		I want credit life insurance.	Signature:
Credit Disability		I want credit disability insurance.	Signature:
Credit Life and Disability		I want credit life and disability insurance.	Signature:

INSURANCE: The following insurance is required to obtain credit:
☐ Credit life insurance ☐ Credit disability ☑ Property insurance ☐ Flood insurance
You may obtain the insurance from anyone you want that is acceptable to creditor
☑ If you purchase ☑ property ☐ flood insurance from creditor you will pay $ for a one year term.
SECURITY: You are giving a security interest in:
☑ The goods or property being purchased   ☐ Real property you already own.
FILING FEES: $ **15.00**
LATE CHARGE: If a payment is more than **15** days late, you will be charged **5.000** % of the principal and interest overdue
PREPAYMENT: If you pay off early, you
☐ may ☑ will not have to pay a penalty.
☐ may ☑ will not be entitled to a refund of part of the finance charge.
ASSUMPTION: Someone buying your property
☐ may ☐ may, subject to conditions ☑ may not assume the remainder of your loan on the original terms.
See your contract documents for any additional information about nonpayment, default, any required repayment in full before the scheduled date and prepayment refunds and penalties
☐ * means an estimate ☐ all dates and numerical disclosures except the late payment disclosures are estimates.

* * NOTE: The Payments shown above include reserve deposits for Mortgage Insurance (if applicable), but exclude Property Taxes and Insurance.

THE UNDERSIGNED ACKNOWLEDGES RECEIVING A COMPLETED COPY OF THIS DISCLOSURE.

_____   (Applicant)   (Date)   _____   (Applicant)   (Date)

_____   (Applicant)   (Date)   _____   (Applicant)   (Date)

_____   (Lender)   (Date)

Calyx Form - til.hp (02/95)

Reprinted with permission from Cherrywood Home Loans, LLC, Denver, Colorado.

After application for a mortgage, avoid making any major purchase until after you move into your new home.

before closing. This potential update provides an excellent reason to hold off buying that boat you've wanted.

Besides the credit report, the lender confirms details you provide on the application with verification forms. You sign verification forms covering employment, deposits, and your mortgage company or landlord. These forms authorize the entities you list to answer the same questions that appear on your application. Their answers and yours should match (see also Figure 2.1).

Appraisal

To calculate the maximum loan amount possible, the lender orders an appraisal. The appraiser examines the house plans, reviews comparable homes in the area, and determines the fair market value of your completed home. The appraised value and the sales price are usually close. If they are different, the lender will calculate the maximum loan amount on the lower figure. Appraisal costs vary, but $250 to $400 is common.

Locks

A loan lock is a promise the lender makes to provide a loan to you at a quoted (locked) rate if your loan is approved. Until you lock your loan rate, the interest rate for your mortgage can go up or down. Loan locks obligate the lender for a set time ranging from 7 to as many as 270 days. Longer locks may come with a fee. To obtain the locked rate, both the approval of the application and the closing must occur before the lock expires.

You can lock in a rate when you apply, during processing, when the loan is approved, or anytime after approval. You must time the decision to lock your loan rate with exceptional care because rate changes affect your monthly payment. For buyers with housing or debt ratios near the limit, a slight increase in the mortgage payment can mean their loans are denied.

You may be tempted to lock when rates are favorable, but locking too soon can cause panic at the end of construction. Pressuring a builder to complete a home so you can beat a lock expiration may result in rushed work and poor quality. The best approach provides a clear view of your financial circumstances from the beginning and allows a margin for safety in your numbers.

When you are ready to lock your loan, notify the lender in writing and request confirmation in writing. Conversations are difficult to prove later if errors occur. You should know the following information about your loan lock:

- What is locked—the rate, the points, or both?
- Can the rate increase at all?
- If rates decrease, do you benefit?
- Does the lock carry a charge?
- If the lock expires, is a second lock available?
- If so, will you be charged a second fee?
- Is the lock fee refundable, and if so, under what circumstances?
- Is the lock voidable, and if so, under what circumstances?

Loan Approval

When you apply for a loan, your lender estimates the time needed to obtain approval. Add a week to that estimate and expect some last-minute details to need your attention. For example, your lender may request a letter explaining information in your financial history. Several weeks after that first meeting, you should receive loan approval as evidenced by a loan commitment. This loan approval should state clearly, in writing—

- that you have been approved
- the loan amount, type, and rate
- the period for which the loan is valid
- any conditions of approval, or contingencies, such as closing on the sale of a previous home

Your final approval comes only after you resolve any contingencies. Custom builders usually need a written loan commitment before construction begins. Production builders often work on a home to the point that it is ready for carpet; then put the house on hold until the loan is approved.

Construction Loan

This second type of loan involved in building a home is closely related to the permanent mortgage. The construction loan pays for materials and labor during construction. These loans carry a higher interest rate than permanent financing. The rate usually is based on the prime rate plus a set percentage, commonly 1 to 2 percent. However, interest charges apply only on the amount the lender transfers to the construction account from the date it is transferred. The cost of construction interest starts out low and becomes more significant as the home nears completion. Lenders usually lend up to 70 or 80 percent of the lesser of appraised value or hard costs. Hard costs include permits, materials, and labor. Construction loans seldom cover the costs of builder supervision and margin.

When the builder owns the lot, as is the case with a production builder, he or she arranges construction financing. A record of successful closings combined with a signed purchase agreement for the proposed home convinces the lender to approve construction financing in the builder's name. In such cases the home buyers apply only for their permanent financing. Lenders sometimes want assurance that a permanent mortgage loan is approved to repay the construction loan when the home is complete. For this reason, the lender may require proof that the home buyer has a permanent loan before granting the construction loan.

Streamline or Express Loans

If you own the new home site, you're responsible for both the construction and mortgage loans. When collecting information from potential lenders, ask whether they offer a program that streamlines the application process. Sometimes called an express program, it allows you to apply and qualify for permanent and construction financing in one step. You can obtain these loans from two different lenders, but working with just one simplifies the process, saves time, and reduces fees. The cost savings might cover that jetted tub you've been thinking about.

Application

Regardless of who applies for the construction loan, the lender might require any or all of the items listed in Figure 2.7. Developing these materials involves your architect or design-builder, perhaps an interior designer, and of course, you (Figure 2.8). The construction loan applicant should expect to pay closing costs on the construction loan. When the construction loan closes, work on your new home can begin.

Figure 2.7 Construction Loan Application Checklist

Loan Application Form

Credit Report

Permanent Financing Information

Site Information

☐ Legal description
☐ Plot plan, survey with easements and access
☐ Site status

—Copy of contract to purchase site
—Subordination agreement, if applicable
—Status of taxes
—Status of title

☐ Zoning, appropriate approval letters
☐ Soil report
☐ Utilities, letter of availability
☐ Permits

—Well
—Septic
—Driveway
—Building

☐ Home owners association documents

Home Plans

☐ Blueprints

—Floor plans
—Elevations

—Structural
—Mechanical
—Electrical
—Grading
—Landscaping

☐ Specifications, details of finish work and materials
☐ Appraisal (as if completed)
☐ Construction budget
☐ Construction schedule

Builder Information

☐ Copy of contract with builder
☐ Evidence of earnest money deposit
☐ Resume on builder

—Financial statement
—Trade and financial references
—Other construction work in progress

☐ List of trade contractors and suppliers

—Primary and alternates
—Work and credit references

☐ Evidence of insurance

—Builder's risk or home owner's insurance
—Workers' compensation and general liability insurance
—Flood insurance, if applicable

**Figure 2.8
Filling Out
Construction
Loan Application
Documents**

Draws

The procedure for paying the bills during construction is called a construction draw. The details outlined in the loan documents vary, but generally the steps are as follows:

- Trade contractors and suppliers submit invoices as work progresses.
- The builder approves the invoices. The lender may also want you to approve them.
- The builder makes out checks to pay the approved invoices.
- The approved invoices and checks are presented to the lender with a summary. This collection is called the draw request.
- Upon receipt of a draw request, the lender orders a jobsite inspection.
- The lender compares the expenditures listed to the budget. Where a variance exists, the lender expects an explanation, such as a change order.
- Once everything is approved, inspected, and explained, the lender funds the draw request by depositing money into the construction checking account.
- Depending on the lender's policy, either the lender or the builder mails the checks.

A lien waiver provides added protection for the lender, the builder, and most importantly, the home buyer.

Checks drawn on the construction loan account may have lien waivers printed on the back. By endorsing the check, the payee signs the lien waiver. For more information on liens, review Figure 2.9.

Normally six to eight draws occur during construction of a house, approximately one a month. Lender processing takes from a few days to a week or more, so trade contractors and suppliers should know the cutoff dates and processing time for draws. If an invoice arrives after a cutoff date, the builder usually holds it until the next draw request.

Figure 2.9 Mechanics' Liens

A mechanic's lien is a statutory creation designed to protect the people or firms who have contributed to a construction project but have not been paid. It is a form of security for payment of a debt, a lien on the real estate where the work was performed or the materials supplied. A mechanic's lien is nearly as old as this country. The first such law was passed in the state of Maryland in 1791. Today all the states have a mechanic's lien law.

Who is entitled to a mechanic's lien? Every person or firm who contributes to a construction project is entitled to one, including builders, contractors, trade contractors, suppliers, architects, and laborers.

A mechanic's lien is recorded with the real property records in the county where the jobsite is located. It serves as notice to prospective purchasers, lenders, and other creditors that a lien is on the property for money owed. A mechanic's lien is usually given priority from the date that construction commences, regardless of when it is filed. All mechanics' liens for a specific project normally share priority equally, no matter who files first.

Filing requirements vary from state to state. Usually the person originating the lien must give written notice to the owner of the real estate and any mortgage lender before filing can occur. The states also impose time limits for these notices. After properly serving the notices, the person or company not paid may file the mechanic's lien with the clerk of the court who files and maintains deeds and land records. The court will sometimes provide its own forms for filing.

If filing alone doesn't result in payment, the unpaid person or company must file a law suit to perfect the mechanic's lien. This action is called foreclosure or a suit to enforce a mechanic's lien. If the suit is not filed within a period of time specified by state law, the mechanic's lien is automatically released, whether or not payment has been received.

To avoid missteps that could result in the enforcement of a mechanic's lien, home buyers should familiarize themselves with the law before they authorize the start of construction on a new house. They should know all time limit, notice, and filing requirements so they can keep their new houses out of jeopardy.

Insurance

Lenders require several types of insurance as part of the construction loan package. Builder's risk or home owner's insurance protects the work in progress against liability and damage such as fire, theft, or vandalism. If you own the lot, your home owner's policy may provide the needed coverage. Explore this possibility in detail with your insurance agent.

Workers' compensation insurance protects those who work on the site against on-the-job injury. If you own the lot, it protects you from liability if claims are made. Each trade contractor should provide the builder with proof of this coverage. If trade contractors do not have their own policies, they could leave the builder or home buyer liable for the cost of coverage or results of injuries.

Arranging to pay for your new home is probably one of the least exciting aspects of the home building process. However, the time and thought you invest in this task is vital to your peace of mind, your ability to complete the project successfully, and the long-term return on your investment. The understanding you gain from a careful examination of your financial picture prepares you for all the new home decisions you are going to make.

Selecting a Builder

"I Have a Friend in the Construction Business"

3

Building a home has become a complicated task requiring specialized knowledge and skills. Years ago when a pioneer family wanted a new home, they gathered some nearby neighbors and trees. The men put the house up while the women prepared an abundant feast. By sundown the new home was complete, if not fancy. Now residential construction demands so much knowledge that a carefully selected builder is your best ally in this process.

Selecting the right builder for your new home is akin to choosing the right surgeon when you need an operation. Not only must your builder have knowledge and skills, but your personalities should work well together. Tempted to serve as your own general contractor? Rent the video, *Mr. Blandings Builds His Dream House*. The mishaps in *Mr. Blandings* are entertaining as long as they're happening to Cary Grant—not to you and your checkbook.

Professional Builders

Technological developments as well as quality and service revolutions have affected residential construction. Staying informed about environmental issues, human health and safety concerns, the pros and cons of an increasing variety of building materials, efficient building techniques, and design trends while managing a business, creating a quality product, and servicing customers requires a commitment many of us would label as passionate. Figure 3.1 lists skills professional builders can contribute to the construction of your new home.

Your Ideal Builder

Builders come in all shapes and sizes, just as customers do. Home building firms can have from one to hundreds of employees. Some buyers prefer the security a large corporate establishment represents. Others prefer the personal attention and family feeling of small companies. The type of home you want also influences the type of organization you select.

To select a builder, begin by thinking about yourself. What kind of customer are you? Some companies emphasize straightforward business operations and tight cost controls. Others are service legends who cater to your every whim—with prices set accordingly. If you have purchased or built other homes, recall which aspects of those experiences you enjoyed most—and least. What would you like to repeat? Avoid?

Figure 3.1 What a Professional Builder Can Offer You

Business Skills

- [ ] Negotiates and complies with contracts
- [ ] Develops the information required to obtain a construction loan
- [ ] Maintains a supplier and trade contractor network
- [ ] Prepares estimates and budgets
- [ ] Prepares schedules
- [ ] Documents details accurately
- [ ] Controls costs

Construction

- [ ] Creates a community atmosphere
- [ ] Offers home designs that—

    —Provide interior, exterior appeal
    —Demonstrate energy efficiency
    —Produce healthy and environmentally friendly homes

- [ ] Keeps sites clean, secure, and safe
- [ ] Consistently applies quality standards
- [ ] Provides attention to details, including—

    —Craftsmanship
    —Code compliance

Customer Communications

- [ ] Provides overview
- [ ] Prices selections and options fairly
- [ ] Explains change request procedures
- [ ] Discusses schedule throughout the process
- [ ] Plans meetings that include an offer to tour the site and answer questions
- [ ] Volunteers information and suggestions
- [ ] Meets commitments
- [ ] Enforces the agreed-upon quality standards
- [ ] Delivers promised details

Service

- [ ] Provides a planned orientation, including demonstration of the home's equipment, appliances, and features
- [ ] Provides a written warranty
- [ ] Gives guidance for home maintenance provided or makes it available
- [ ] Provides organized procedures for correcting warranty items in a timely manner

A key issue is deciding which type of product best meets your needs. Builders and their products fall into three broad categories: production, semi-custom, and custom. After listening to customers and observing that flexibility sells homes, production builders have become more amenable to moderate plan changes. Computer-aided design (CAD) systems make plan revisions easier and faster. These developments are blurring the distinctions between the three types of builders.

Clearly you will invest a considerable amount of time, emotion, and money in this purchase no matter which type of builder you select. Careful consideration at this point can assure the right choice for you. While exceptions to the following descriptions exist, these three will give you a general perspective.

Production Builders

Production builders organize their companies for high-volume construction. Local production builders might build as few as 20 homes per year, national firms as many as several thousand. Production builders offer a collection of floor plans, each with a choice of two or more exterior designs or elevations.

Tour model homes to view the different choices. These models, which often are furnished, are also called show homes, display homes, or samples. Buyers can personalize the floor plan they choose by selecting floor coverings, tile, countertops, light fixtures, cabinets, and exterior finishes. The builder may display samples of the choices in the model center or in one centralized and permanent location. Builders refer to these sites as the decorator, selection, or design center.

Adding features from a list of popular options can further personalize the home. Examples include air-conditioning, upgraded appliances, covered patio, mirrored closet doors, tub enclosures, integrated security system wiring, or ceiling fans. Today most production builders accept requests for minor plan changes, such as enlarging a closet or adding a window.

Advantages. To assure your satisfaction, your personal standards should coincide with those of the builder. Models you can view at leisure provide an opportunity to study the quality of the builder's work and get a feel of the home that blueprints alone cannot achieve. Having a standardized list of choices and options means it's faster and easier to make selections. The cost of your combination of selections is known quickly—sometimes immediately—making it easier to finalize your decisions.

Through repetition, the builder has worked any bugs out of floor plans. The total time to build is usually shorter than with a new design because construction personnel are familiar with the plans. Suppliers stock regularly used items, making material delays less likely. High-volume work, such as occurs in a subdivision, offers an advantage in scheduling trade contractors and can result in significant cost savings. A well-planned and well-built subdivision often is extremely prestigious. Most communities include entryways designed to convey image and amenities such as a pool or tennis courts.

Disadvantages. Excitement over your new home may turn to frustration as you peruse the builder's prepared floor plans and approved collection of colors and materials. The available choices may not include a combination that is just right for you. Altering the structural elements—those components that support the weight of the home, such as the foundation walls—requires re-engineering and resubmission of plans to the building department. These expensive and time-consuming steps disrupt the momentum of high-volume construction. Consequently, production builders permit few structural changes.

Other purchasers have your floor plan and elevation. Although production builders plan product mix within a community and monitor exterior color choices, two similar homes can end up near each other. Although you can examine the quality of the builder's work in the models, little room exists for negotiating individual standards. Production builders usually work in subdivisions where they own the lots rather than on individual sites. If you want one of their homes, you must select a site in one of their subdivisions.

Custom Builders

These builders specialize in starting with a blank sheet of paper or computer screen and creating a unique home. You can also review existing floor plans and draw ideas from those. Custom builders tend to be small companies, both in the number of homes they build each year (typically 10 or fewer) and the number of employees in their companies.

Some custom builders establish relationships with one or more independent architects for plan development. For others, called design/build firms, the builder is also an architect or has an architect or draftsperson on staff. Working with one firm allows you to develop one relationship and simplifies communication. Jack Drake, owner of Drake Homes in St. Charles, Missouri, says, "During a relationship that lasts 15 months to 3 years, the design/build firm focuses on the client's needs and desires. First [they] help create their dream on paper, then in the real world." Drake observes, "The design/build builder is really in the people business, the product just happens to be a home."

Advantages. Custom builders create one-of-a-kind homes. They design their operations around the customer's active involvement throughout the building process. You learn a great deal about home construction. If you enjoy the education, you will find this process rewarding in itself.

Custom builders have experience with a wide variety of finishes, unusual treatments, and design details. Often they have established relationships with trade contractors who perform specialized work, such as stained glass insets or copper roofing. Their systems and personnel are organized to build on isolated, scattered sites.

Disadvantages. Expect a significant initial investment in time and dollars for design development and the creation of working blueprints and specifications. Meetings can take many hours, followed by more meetings that take more hours. This process is not one to rush. The preliminary stages can take months of changing the plans and then changing the changes. Since alterations are possible throughout the process and choices are virtually unlimited, costs can rise dramatically unless the buyer has the self-discipline to stick to the intended budget.

Again, because of the unique nature of each home, you lose the economies that large-volume builders achieve. Custom-built homes typically take the longest to complete. Supervising scattered site work combined with the longer time needed to build one-of-a-kind homes also increases costs.

Semi-Custom Builders

These builders combine the characteristics of production and custom building. They work with preexisting plans, each with many possible variations. Semi-custom builders are flexible regarding changes, including those that require engineering and building department approval. Consequently, although you begin with an existing floor plan, many more opportunities exist for you to alter that plan.

Advantages. Many buyers have difficulty visualizing floor plans but have definite ideas about what they want in their homes. They feel more comfortable starting with a plan that is close to what they want than with a blank page or computer screen. Revising existing plans is normally faster and less costly than creating a new set of blueprints, yet this option still provides an opportunity for extensive changes. Semi-custom builders are flexible about building location, working on individual sites, or in subdivisions that include the work of several builders.

Disadvantages. Fine-tuning a house plan takes time and money. You lose the economies of large-volume work and the resulting prices. Crews need more time when building from unfamiliar plans. Semi-custom builders are more open to plan changes than production builders before construction begins but less willing than custom builders to accept changes once construction is under way.

Which Type for You?

Can an existing plan satisfy your new home needs and desires? Do you have lifestyle circumstances to accommodate, such as a parent who lives with you? Do you make up your

By considering what kind of buyer you are, you can develop a more accurate description of your ideal builder.

mind and that's it, or will you reconsider and make adjustments throughout the process? How much construction knowledge do you have? Are you interested in learning more? Do you have the time and interest to involve yourself in the day-to-day decisions about your home? How quickly do you want or need to move?

One caution to keep in mind: don't risk hiring a builder who operates in one style, thinking that you can coax, cajole, nag, bribe, or threaten the company to alter its culture. Each company's business style is shaped by the philosophies, personalities, and goals of the people associated with it. Their attitudes, systems, procedures, and even their documents are designed around them. Believing you can change all that can result in frustration, conflict, and dissatisfaction.

Avoid purchasing a production home with the idea that you will talk the builder into making what is for that builder an unusual number of changes. Neither should you believe that a custom builder can complete a custom home in the same time frame that a production company requires for its most popular plan. Clarify in your mind which type will best serve your goals and look for that one.

Labels Do Not Equal Quality

Whether a home is categorized as production, semi-custom, or custom neither indicates nor guarantees its quality. Avoid getting tangled in misplaced perceptions about the prestige attached to labels. Look for a builder who can meet your needs at the level of quality you find appealing. What is the builder noted for? What is the hallmark of the organization? What is the first thing people think of when they hear the name? Design? Locations? Attention to detail? Energy-saving features? Service? Decide which of these are important to you, and look for an organization with values and priorities that parallel your own.

This research takes time, but nothing outweighs selecting the right builder. Everyone will offer advice on finding the right builder. Keep in mind that your ideal builder is not necessarily the same one your parents or best friend would select. Consider everyone's input, but remember that ultimately this choice and the resulting home are yours.

Finding Potential Builders

Begin your search by discovering who is building in the area where you want to live. Creating a list of potential builders is fairly easy; selecting one is a bit tougher. Start with a preliminary list of candidates from a variety of sources, and focus on builders with experience in your style and price range.

Professional Organizations and Licensing Boards

Local chapters of the National Association of Home Builders (NAHB) can provide a list of member companies. While membership in this professional organization is an indication of interest in continuing education and professional development, you should follow through on the suggestions elsewhere in this chapter for checking out the candidates.

Not all areas require builder licensing, and those that do vary widely in their requirements. Determine how builders become and stay licensed in your jurisdiction by phoning the builder licensing board and asking what is required to obtain a license. This contact is another source of names and not a substitute for your own investigation.

Advertising

Newspaper, radio, and even television advertising provide an obvious source of builder information. Look for community feature articles in small, regional publications that can help you get to know an unfamiliar area. You can quickly scan information about prices, locations, product styles, and sizes to identify potential candidates. Consider this information as a starting point. Paying for an ad or submitting a press release does not guarantee quality or service. Some of the best builders rely on referrals from their home owners and do not advertise.

Word-of-Mouth

Talk to friends, relatives, and the folks at work. Ask people who have recently built homes about their builder. Veteran customers are good sources of information on construction quality and customer treatment.

Real Estate Agents

Real estate agents familiar with new home construction locally can provide builder names and insights into quality and customer satisfaction. Be certain the agent you speak to is familiar with new construction in your target area.

Exploring on Your Own

Drive around. As simple as this idea sounds, it offers the added advantage of helping you become familiar with communities and homes in progress. You may find the perfect site at the same time you discover your ideal builder. Note the name of builders whose work you find appealing. Visit communities on a Saturday morning and talk to home owners as they wash their cars, walk their dogs, or shovel snow (Figure 3.2). This last group will appreciate the interruption.

Long-Distance Moves

Moving a long distance from your current residence makes the task more challenging. Traveling back and forth can add to the costs and the timetable. The offerings of production builders or a home built on speculation by a semi-custom builder may meet your scheduling needs if a new job is waiting. Renting can relieve some of the pressure and allow you to proceed at a less frantic pace. Another possibility is working with a relocation service.

Checking Out the Builders

Now comes the important task of narrowing your list of potential builders down to one. While compiling your list you saw the offerings of a number of builders and probably

**Figure 3.2
Talk to Residents
in Areas Where
You Might Want
to Live**

eliminated some of them based on size, design, or price. Now you can take a closer look at remaining candidates.

Look at Their Homes

Look closely at each builder's finished work and work in progress. Your home will receive the same attention to detail (Figure 3.3). Notice the quality of site management. Construction sites are intrinsically messy. It takes effort to keep them clean and under control. Are the homes and materials reasonably protected from weather, traffic damage, and theft? Take note of personnel you encounter. What are their attitudes toward you, each other, and the product they are creating?

Meet the Builder

Ask about things that are important to you and get a sense of the company's personality. Think of this as interviewing the company. When you visit the builder's office or the sales office, do you feel comfortable? Ask to meet the person who would be in charge of build-

**Figure 3.3
An Outside
Stairway Displays
a Builder's Quality**

Photo by James F. Wilson, Dallas, Texas.

ing your home. What experience does he or she have? Which building code applies in this area? How well is it enforced? Ask about turnover. Excessive changes in staff and trade contractors create opportunities for missed details. Look at floor plans and talk about the home you want. How well does this company listen? Are the builder's suggestions and comments helpful and relevant? Are your questions answered clearly and completely?

Ask for an Overview

Many builders today provide a home owner manual that guides buyers through the process and serves as a reference after move-in. Does the company schedule a preconstruction conference to review your plans and the process just before starting construction? Whom would you contact with questions? Are there routine points at which you are invited to tour your home and have the company's undivided attention to discuss questions? What is the policy on change orders? What guidelines does the company use to determine a delivery date? Many factors outside the builder's control can cause delays, and builders who promise a firm date too early often disappoint their buyers. Every builder should have a system for updating you on the targeted delivery date. (See Carol Smith, *Homeowner Manual: A Template for Home Builders,* 2nd ed.)

Large companies may host one or more home buyer seminars during the process. If this situation is the case with a builder you are considering, ask to sit in on one. Such programs cover basic information and give home buyers an opportunity to get to know the builder's staff and their future neighbors. This investment of resources usually is a sign that the company is working hard to communicate with buyers.

Read Documents

Ask to see the contract documents and warranty, and take blank copies home. Pay close attention to sample specifications and written warranty standards. Consider whether the builder's chosen materials and methods appeal to you. Also note the amount of detail provided; details demonstrate how precise the builder is in communicating. You can usually expect this same attention to detail to flow through the construction of your home.

References

Impressed by that four-color magazine ad? Are you imagining yourself watching the sun set behind that cozy home nestled on a quiet street? Back to reality. Ads and signs merely alert you to the fact that a builder exists; they do not establish how the company treats its customers. For the answer to that important question, you must talk to the customers themselves.

> **Call some of the builder's previous buyers or drive through an area where the builder has been working.**

Home Owners. Call some of the builder's previous buyers or drive through an area where the builder has been working. Finding and talking with custom builder clients may require a bit of time. If the idea seems awkward at first, practice these words, "I'm considering having [name of builder] build my home. Can I ask you a few questions about your home and how you were treated?" Unless you happen to connect with the community recluse, you'll gain a wealth of information. Talk to at least five people and visit several areas if possible.

Few builders will send you to the customer they failed to satisfy, but random conversations may identify one. A single negative incident may result from an honest misunderstanding or a personality conflict. If the problem occurred because the buyer was turned down on a warranty request, do not panic. In fact, beware of builders who do anything and everything for their buyers. Future customers, like you, pay for all those extras. However, if you hear again and again about unfulfilled promises, quality that disappoints expectations, lack of follow-through on orientation items, or slow or no warranty service, move on. Your search for the right builder is not yet over.

Building Departments and Consumer Protection Entities. Building inspectors or departments are unlikely to provide you with much information unless you have a close friend who works there with whom you can chat. Similarly, entities such as state and local consumer protection agencies and the Better Business Bureau can report only what's on record. They cannot recommend or evaluate. However, if you hear that numerous complaints are on file, exercise caution.

Many factors must come together correctly for you to feel comfortable with your builder. Price is certainly one, although what initially seems like the best deal may not be. Consider the comments in Figure 3.4 on the cost-per-square-foot trap. Scheduling is

---

Figure 3.4 The Cost-Per-Square-Foot Trap

Your new home's cost-per-square-foot is an interesting number to know. Calculate it after you have made all your decisions, the specifications are finalized, and the builder has provided you with accurate pricing obtained from suppliers and trade contractors. Accurate pricing requires specifications and input from suppliers and trade contractors. Done properly, the process can take weeks. Until the builder completes that process the cost-per-square-foot figure is a conversation tidbit, not a criteria for selecting your builder.

Buyers who do not understand the complexity of this process and the importance of clearly written specifications sometimes take their blueprints from builder to builder requesting price quotes. They may hire the builder who said their 4-bedroom, 3-bath home could be built for $68 a square foot, only to discover too late that this price includes 2x4, not 2x6 framing, excludes tree removal, and that the countertops are laminate, not tile. The builder made assumptions and quoted a price; the buyers made different assumptions and accepted it.

Selecting a builder based on cost per square foot is like choosing a car based on price per pound or a restaurant on cost per calorie. Decide on a builder based on all the information you gather and be certain you know exactly what comes with all those square feet you are paying for.

another powerful consideration. Then add the equally important quality, location, design, and willingness to accommodate your special needs and wants.

Throughout your explorations and conversations, visits and revisits, you no doubt heard the same names again and again. Comparing one detail after the next, you keep coming back to the same builder. Phone calls are returned promptly; questions are answered completely; information is forthright and clear. Suggestions about the home you want make sense; the chemistry feels right. You're more excited than ever to get started. The price range is in line with your budget and the school district appeals to your children. Your hard work has paid off; you have found your builder.

Contracts and Agreements

"Who Writes This Stuff?"

4

Whereas the party of the first part hereinafter witnesseth. . . ." Is anything more confounding than contract legalese? Written by and passed down through generations of attorneys and judges, these time-tested phrases, already interpreted in the courts, have predictable meanings. Rewording them into every-day English would require reinterpretation, so rather than risk surprises in court, we just endure the legalese. Read the documents associated with planning and building your home. It's tedious work. If it is too tedious for you, ask your attorney to review them. If you have questions, get answers before you sign anything.

Contracts vary in form, length, content, and print size. Expect standard elements such as the names of the parties, dates, and signatures to show up in every contract. Avoid complacency with boilerplate or standard paragraphs. Read and understand everything you sign. Contracts contain clauses that address company experiences and regional items. In this chapter we highlight the common elements of two agreements, a design agreement and a purchase agreement.

Design Agreement

Before you build a semi-custom or custom home you need assistance in designing it. A design, preconstruction, or professional services agreement, such as the one shown in Figure 4.1, outlines this part of the process. It defines the working relationship between you and your designer or architect. This agreement describes the steps followed to create your home plans, but it does not commit you to build the home. Typically three phases are listed: design schematics, preliminary design, and working drawings.

You meet with the design team to review each phase of the work and discuss desired refinements before proceeding to the next level of detail. Each phase may require one or more meetings. Between meetings you make choices, list questions, and continue to imagine your new home. Remember to filter your ideas through the reality of that budget total from Chapter 2.

Design Schematics

The design process begins with rough sketches, called schematics, drawn at 1/8-inch scale. Each 1/8 inch represents a foot, and therefore a wall that will be 8 feet long when the framers build it appears as 1 inch on these sketches. These drawings reflect your discus-

Figure 4.1 Sample Design Agreement

This preconstruction agreement is made this _____ day of _____ , 200 ____ , between

_____ , the Client, who resides at _____ ,

and the [builder] , whose principal place of business is at _____ .

The Client and the [builder] agree as set forth below:

Project: _____ [describe in detail] _____

This project is designed to fall within a budget range of $ _____ to $ _____ for construction.

1. **Furnishing Design.** The [builder] shall furnish the design of the project in accordance with the following phases:

   Phase 1. Based upon the Client's project requirements, the [builder] will provide design schematics, including field measurements. These schematics are to assist the Client in determining the feasibility of the project.

   Phase 2. Upon approval of the design schematics, the [builder] will proceed with preliminary design development, floor plan, and elevations. Unless otherwise noted, drawings will be to scale.

   Phase 3. From approved preliminary design documents, the [builder] will provide working drawings and specifications. These working drawings will serve as the basis for the [builder's] estimate of the cost of construction and for the construction of the project.

2. **Payment Schedule.** In return for the foregoing services, the Client agrees to pay the [builder] as follows:

   Phase 1. Compensation for phase 1 shall be in the amount of _____ dollars ($ _____),

   and the payment is due on _____ .

   Phase 2. Compensation for phase 2 shall be in the amount of _____ dollars ($ _____),

   and the payment is due on _____ .

   Phase 3. Compensation for phase 3 shall be in the amount of _____ dollars ($ _____),

   and the payment is due on _____ .

3. **Engineering and Other Extra Fees.** The [builder] anticipates that the scope of the project will

   require the services of an engineer. The Client shall pay the engineering fees at _____

   _____ dollars ($ _____) per hour, up to a maximum cost of ($ _____).

   The [builder] shall not be responsible for the payment of any engineering fees.

4. **Failure to Proceed.** If the Client elects not to proceed after any phase, the [builder] is entitled to payment in accordance with paragraph 2.

Figure 4.1 Sample Design Agreement (*Continued*)

5. Change in Work. If the scope of the work or the manner of its execution is materially changed, the additional work shall be billed on an hourly basis at the following rates:

The [builder] at _____ dollars ($ _____)

The engineer at _____ dollars ($ _____)

Others _____ [list them] _____ at _____ dollars ($ _____).

6. Ownership of the Documents. The preliminary design documents, working drawings, and specifications are for the sole use of the [builder or remodeler] in connection with this project, and they shall remain the property of the [builder]. They are not to be used by the Client or any third party on other projects without the written consent of the [builder]. The Client will be liable to the [builder] for all losses arising out of the unauthorized use or sale of these copyrighted documents.

7. Client Cooperation. The Client will provide full information regarding the Client's requirements for the project and make necessary decisions required for completion of design documents in a timely manner.

8. Delivery of Estimated Costs. The [builder] shall complete the design phase and provide the Client with the cost to construct the project by the _____ day of _____, 200 ___ .

9. Client's Right of Rescission. Pursuant to federal law you have three (3) days from [signature date] to rescind this agreement. Client acknowledges receipt of two (2) copies of the notice of the right of rescission.

Client _____ Date _____

Client _____ Date _____

Builder _____ Date _____

Disclaimer. The sample contracts and clauses shown in this book are provided for educational purposes in order to illustrate the principles discussed. They should not be used as forms. These contracts are designed to cover the major topics of consideration for most new residential construction contracts. However, the contract provisions shown do not and cannot apply to every situation, nor do they comply with any particular state law. Some of the provisions will not apply to a particular situation, while in other cases additional terms may be appropriate. Laws can vary, and some states may require specific language and formats for certain contracts. New home buyers should work with their builders and attorneys to prepare documents that meet their particular needs.

Reprinted from David Crump and David S. Jaffe, Contracts and Liability, *5th ed. (Washington, D.C.: BuilderBooks.com, National Association of Home Builders, 2003), p. 176-77.*

sions with the designer about style, size, and layout. Informal drawings show how the proposed home fits on the lot and suggest an elevation or exterior design. Do not expect polished, detailed drawings or precise measurements at this point. However, you can see the home you described beginning to take shape. You will, no doubt, make changes—moving rooms around, adjusting their sizes, adding closets, or a deck.

Preliminary Design

Incorporating your comments about the schematic design, the design team redraws the home, typically at 1/4-inch scale. These larger drawings show more detail in both floor plan and elevations. At meetings expect to discuss materials and their relative costs while you continue to make decisions and changes and ask questions.

Working Drawings

The builder can price and build from the final-stage plans, called working drawings (Figure 4.2). These plans include fully dimensioned drawings, sections (drawings that show the interior details for constructing walls, stairs, and floors), and details required for the building permit. Besides the floor plans and elevations, working drawings include a foundation plan, electrical details, cabinet layouts, and framing layouts for floors, walls, and roof. Together you and the design team will review your requested changes and the final specifications. Chapter 6 includes an example of specifications. The builder then obtains prices from trade contractors and prepares a budget.

    The design agreement also lists the cost and payment schedule for each step of this process. Some preconstruction agreements require you to authorize and pay for a soil test or other expenses necessary to determine the structure and price of your home (Figure 4.3). The design agreement also spells out who owns the completed plans and who pays for the services of outside professionals such as an engineer.

    If you build a production home, your builder will have completed all this work before you see the plans. However you arrive at a final design, once there you are ready to build your home. The contract for this commitment, often called a purchase agreement, is longer than a design agreement.

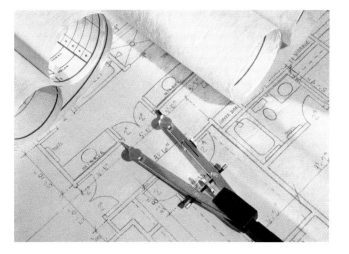

**Figure 4.2
Working Drawings**

Purchase Agreement

When we talk about the contract for the purchase of a new home, we refer to a collection of documents. These items may include the purchase agreement itself, blueprints, specifications, option and color selection sheets, lighting schedule, site drawing, and limited war-

**Figure 4.3
Will Your Dream
Home Fit Your
Lot?**

Photo by James F. Wilson, Dallas, Texas.

ranty. The purchase agreement mentions each of these documents and by reference makes them part of your legal agreement with the builder. Besides drawing this collection together, the core agreement includes many common clauses such as those briefly described in the pages that follow. Figure 4.4 provides a checklist of the usual items in a purchase agreement.

Price

Builders use two basic methods to price homes: fixed-price and cost plus. With fixed-price, both you and the builder know the cost of the home described in the plans. That price is the one you pay unless you and the builder agree to changes later. The other method is cost plus. "Plus *what*?" you may ask. The "plus," a percentage of the cost of building the home, goes to the builder for overhead and profit. The percentage is fixed, but the dollar amount may change, depending on material prices and decisions you make during construction.

Production builders price homes using the fixed-price method. Custom builders use either fixed-price or cost plus, depending on philosophy and negotiations with individual buyers. Regardless of which approach you use, remember that the options, selections, and changes you request can increase the total cost of your home.

The price of your home and the cost of the options you've selected appear in the purchase agreement, followed by a schedule of payments. A semi-custom or custom home contract includes a draw schedule as determined by the construction lender. A draw schedule sets out the timetable for paying bills during construction (see Chapter 2 for more information on draws).

Allowances. You may find you're ready to get the building process moving but still haven't finalized choices for items like carpet, cabinets, tile, appliances, and light fixtures. And what if the builder cannot determine the exact cost of some aspects of construction

Figure 4.4 Purchase Agreement Checklist

Date

Names of the Parties

Property Identification

Price

☐ Allowances
☐ Reimbursable expenses

Financing

Construction

☐ Commence and complete construction
☐ Change orders
☐ Conformance with plans and
   specifications

—Blueprints (Exhibit ___)
—Specifications (Exhibit ___)
—Color selections (Exhibit ___)
—Options (Exhibit___)
—Lighting schedule (Exhibit ___)
—Soil report, if applicable (Exhibit ___)

☐ Plan ownership
☐ Site visits
☐ Inspection and acceptance
☐ Site clean-up
☐ Mandatory clauses (insulation, for
   example)
☐ Warranty
☐ Home owners association
☐ Settlement
☐ Insurance
☐ Default or termination
☐ Alternative dispute resolution
☐ Co-op broker information
☐ Miscellaneous

—Entire agreement
—Where to send notices
—Balance of contract still applies if one
   clause is found unenforceable
—The terms of the contract survive the
   closing

Signatures of All Parties

in advance, such as the cost of establishing a well? Your contract can include an allowance that estimates the cost of each listed item. That allowance permits you to include this amount in the contract total and therefore your mortgage. If the actual cost of an item exceeds the allowance, you can pay the difference in cash or ask your lender to approve a higher mortgage.

Detailed allowance descriptions minimize confusion and eliminate potential disagreements. Instead of "floor covering, $8,000," the allowance should specify "288 square yards of carpet and pad at $24 per yard installed: $6,912." When you align allowances with your expectations and budget, you minimize your need to come up with cash or increase your loan.

Reimbursable Expenses. Some unforeseeable expenses occur in the construction of every home. If the budget includes a contingency category (usually 2 to 5 percent of the total cost of the home), the builder attributes unforeseen expenses to that category up to the budgeted amount. The reimbursable expense category allows the builder to collect from you for items no one could reasonably foresee that exceed the contingency category. If the budget did not include a contingency, all unforeseen expenses may become yours to pay. Examples of reimbursable expenses include removing a large rock formation encountered when the foundation is dug or addressing groundwater that went undiscovered until work began. These costs are usually determined based on time and materials.

Financing

Unless you are paying cash for your home, you apply for a mortgage shortly after signing the contract. If you own the lot, you apply for the construction loan as well. A standard finance contingency clause protects you in the event you do not qualify for the financing described—a disappointment usually avoided by prequalifying. However, if it does occur, this clause voids the contract and the builder returns your deposit.

Construction

The contract lists the plans, specifications, and buyer selections sheet by name, number of pages, and date. The builder commits to doing this work in a "workmanlike manner" as defined by general practice in the region. Many long conversations have occurred over the definition of "workmanlike manner." Some have taken place in court and made lots of money for the attorneys doing the talking. The contract also covers many details about the construction process.

Commence and Complete Construction. Many builders wait for the buyer's loan approval before beginning to build the home. In most jurisdictions homes are legally complete when the building department issues a certificate of occupancy. This certificate means the home satisfies applicable codes for residential construction in the area.

The big question is how many days pass between these two events. Construction delays that affect the closing date, such as weather, availability of labor and materials, and slow inspections, are sometimes unavoidable. The builder should keep you informed of any delays, however. Some contracts describe the liability for extra expenses that result from avoidable delays caused by either the builder or the buyers.

Conformance with Plans and Specifications. Like the weather, the government, suppliers, and other factors fall outside the builder's control. The conformance with plans and specifications clause allows for minor changes caused by code revisions, site conditions, or other events the builder cannot control. If a supplier goes out of business or a manufacturer changes models, the builder has no choice but to alter the intended home accordingly. "The builder has the right to substitute materials or equipment of equal or better value" appears in nearly every new home contract.

Similarly, the individual handcrafting of each new home makes exact reproduction unlikely. Measurements vary slightly from any model or plans. The exact placement of switches, outlets, and vents changes a bit.

Whether you purchase a production, semi-custom, or custom home, review each detail of the specifications carefully. This portion of the contract documents defines the materials and methods used in building your home. Make sure any detail or item you want included in your home is in the specifications. Adding items later requires a change order and a corresponding change in the price.

Change Orders. Many builders allow buyers to request changes during construction. Wise buyers and builders make no changes without putting the details in writing. You can review a sample change order and detailed information on this important topic in Chapter 8.

Plan Ownership. Production and semi-custom builders own the plans from which they build, even if they allow some custom changes. A few builders will sell a copy, but the cost is usually significant. If you build a custom home, you can negotiate this issue with your

Builders usually do not accept liability for defects in plans unless they have complete control over them.

builder. Settle the point early and document your decision to prevent misunderstandings (see Figure 4.1 Design Agreement).

Site Visits. Although you're anxious to see your home go up, your builder may restrict site visits because of increased safety regulations and insurance liability. Some builders schedule tours of the home as work progresses to give the buyers their undivided attention during these appointments.

Noninterference. Your builder may expect you to visit the site but not to attempt to direct the work in progress. The builder's routine inspections identify items that need correcting. Direct your input to the builder, not the people working on site. Workers have no authority to change anything, and confusion can easily result. Refer to Chapter 8 for more discussion of this subject.

Inspection and Acceptance. You have one last opportunity to review the home just before closing. This final inspection process is spelled out in many contracts. Most builders combine this last inspection with an educational demonstration of your new home. For full details, see Chapter 10, Home Owner Orientation.

Site Clean-Up. The responsibility for keeping the construction site clean and safe lies with the builder and trade contractors. Most contracts state this clearly, and some home owners associations will require a deposit for clean up. Today's builders are stricter than ever about this aspect of the work. A clean site is safer, discourages theft, and encourages pride of workmanship.

Mandatory Clauses

Your contract will contain a number of mandatory clauses, such as an insulation notice. Builders must specify the type, thickness, and R-value of insulation used in your home. This information can appear in the contract or an addendum to the contract. A notice discussing radon, while not required, has become common. Chapter 13 contains more information about radon.

Warranty

Another document usually "incorporated herein by reference" is the new home limited warranty. It is part of the legal agreement between yourself and your builder and therefore a necessary part of the contract. The limited warranty your builder provides defines who is responsible if something goes wrong in your home after closing. Read Chapter 14 and your new home limited warranty carefully. The information is important to your long-term satisfaction with your new home.

Home Owners Association

Unless you already own the lot for your home, the builder's contract will reference the applicable home owners association documents as part of your agreement. These include Covenants, Conditions, and Restrictions, commonly called CC&Rs. If you think contract documents make good reading, you'll love these. Read them anyway. The home owners association requires its design review committee to approve your home plan before construction begins. For more details, see Home Owners Association Regulations in Chapter 7.

Settlement

The settlement clause explains how the builder transfers ownership of the home to you. The Real Estate Settlement Procedures Act (RESPA) may regulate this event if you are receiving a mortgage loan made or insured by an agency of the federal government. Chapter 11, Closing, discusses this subject.

Possession

When the title or escrow company has recorded transfer of title to the property, you can take possession of your new home. You can take possession before this date with a lease, although builders are usually reluctant to provide a lease. In no event can you take possession or move belongings into the home before the builder obtains a certificate of occupancy from the building department.

Insurance

No one likes to see insurance claims occur, but as discussed in Chapter 2, complete insurance coverage for construction work is essential. The contract specifies whether the builder or the home buyer will maintain the needed policies.

Default or Termination

A termination clause defines the circumstances under which either party can terminate the contract and describes the resulting costs. The contract should specify what obligations exist if either party defaults or fails to fulfill its duties under the contract.

Alternative Dispute Resolution

No one plans to have disagreements during construction of a new home, but they can occur. Some contracts address this possibility by providing for arbitration or mediation. In arbitration, each side presents its views and the arbitrator makes a decision. In mediation, a mediator facilitates communication and guides the discussion as the two parties come to their own solution. Either option can prevent court action, at least until the parties have exhausted the method described in the contract. Make sure the contract is clear about whether the result of the alternative dispute resolution is binding.

Co-op Broker

The name and address of your real estate agent may appear in the contract along with the percentage of commission due at closing. An addendum may outline details about the relationship between the real estate agent and the parties to the transaction.

Miscellaneous

Most contracts contain clauses covering standard legalities. The "entire agreement" clause, which says that only what is in writing counts, is one of the most significant. The contract documents should contain all points of agreement. Other miscellaneous clauses might include information such as:

- where to mail notices about the contract
- if one clause is found unenforceable by a court or is waived by either party, the rest of the contract still applies
- that the terms of the contract survive or continue in force after the closing or settlement on the home

Still awake? Now you finally get to sign and date the contract. The meeting to go over all the paperwork and sign everything can take up to several hours. Be prepared. Ask the builder for copies of the documents before this meeting so you can study them, note any questions, and review the documents with your attorney. Whether you do so in advance or during the contract session, make sure you read—and understand—everything before you sign anything. The contract is in force only when all named parties have signed. You are ultimately responsible for your happiness with your new home. A signed contract is legally binding, and no one is sympathetic to the excuse, "I was so excited I wasn't really paying attention."

Location? Location? Location? 5

Somewhere there's a site that's right for you. The question is, where? Perhaps you already own land in an area where you want to live. Even if you love that land, review the Building Site Checklist (Figure 5.1) to prevent any surprises. If the land is unsatisfactory, consider selling or trading it for a more appropriate site.

Select Possible Areas

Unless you already own land, you have an important task ahead of you. Use a good map to identify areas in which you would consider living based on distance to work and other family activities. For most folks, up to 40 minutes to work and 20 minutes to shopping is acceptable. Decide what is acceptable for your family.

Does your lifestyle fit best in an urban, suburban, or rural setting? This choice is a matter of lifestyle and attitudes, not right or wrong. If you are familiar with the region, you'll have an easier time narrowing the areas in which you will look. If you are new to the area, some exploring is in order. Any or all of several types of lots may be available within the areas you ultimately select for exploration.

Individual Sites

Builders refer to an isolated building location as off-site or as a scattered site. The lot is all in one place, but the builder's work is scattered. Individual sites are not always in rural areas. You can find in-fill sites situated among existing homes in urban settings. Urban lots usually have all services available. Established improvements and schools can lower the fees and assessments associated with these lots. On the other hand, fees can rise significantly if area utilities and services need repair or replacement. Make no assumptions based on appearances. Follow through with a complete investigation of any site you consider.

Production builders are not organized to build on scattered sites; their staffing setups are designed for subdivision work. Individual sites are more appropriate for custom or semi-custom builders whose systems evolved for this type of work. Scattered sites are one reason their homes usually cost more.

Figure 5.1 Building Site Checklist

Cost

- [ ] Lot price
- [ ] Property taxes
- [ ] Utility hook-ups
- [ ] Impact fees

Legal Status

- [ ] Zoning (subject to change)
- [ ] Building department
- [ ] Home owners association

    —Covenants
    —Design review

- [ ] Owner
- [ ] Owner's agent
- [ ] Title

Survey

- [ ] Size
- [ ] Boundaries, property corners
- [ ] Easements
- [ ] Setbacks
- [ ] Square-footage requirements
- [ ] Height restrictions
- [ ] Orientation

Fees

- [ ] Permit
- [ ] Home owners association deposits or fees
- [ ] Water tap fee or well cost
- [ ] Sewer tap fee or septic cost
- [ ] Electric hook-up
- [ ] Gas hook-up
- [ ] Phone hook-up
- [ ] Cable TV or satellite service

Unique Construction Factors

- [ ] Access
- [ ] Foundation required for soil conditions
- [ ] Site preparation (trees, rocks, groundwater)
- [ ] Special grading concerns
- [ ] Seasonal weather impact on schedule
- [ ] Ecological concerns
- [ ] Adjacent sites

    —Drainage
    —View
    —Present or future development

Hazards or Negative Concerns

- [ ] Floodplain
- [ ] Weather
- [ ] Seismic zones
- [ ] Crime rate
- [ ] Pollution

Services

- [ ] Government

    —Post office and mail delivery
    —Police and fire protection
    —Road maintenance and snow removal

- [ ] Trash collection
- [ ] Transportation
- [ ] Schools
- [ ] Cultural amenities
- [ ] Medical services
- [ ] Banking, business opportunities
- [ ] Places of worship
- [ ] Recreation

Subdivision Sites

A land developer may develop (provide streets and main utility lines) a group of lots and offer them for sale. One or more builders buy the lots and offer their services to build homes on them. In some cases the developer is also the builder or one of the builders.

If you decide to have your home built in a subdivision, learn who the developer is. Review the quality of the developer's work as carefully as you do your builder's. Look at other subdivisions created by the same firm. Are planned amenities installed on schedule?

Is the community design appealing? Take note of the entry treatment; you will see it often. Is traffic controlled adequately? How are common areas cared for?

A site you consider in a large community may come under the provisions of the federal Interstate Land Sales Full Disclosure Act of 1968. This law requires that developers of large communities (over 50 lots) who work across state lines or use the mail to advertise provide property reports to buyers. These reports provide information on the location and conditions of the community and background on the developer's business and terms of the offer.

Selecting a subdivision site means working with one of the builders operating there. The land and home purchase become a package. You need only one contract, one loan, and one closing. Construction can begin shortly after your lender approves your mortgage and you make necessary selections.

Builder Guidance

Buyers sometimes select their lots before they contact a builder. If you are not committed to a site, getting ideas from your builder could prove beneficial. Your builder may know of sites in your price range with the characteristics needed for your home plan. You need a site that's feasible for the style of home you want, and your builder may notice characteristics that someone with less building experience would overlook. For instance, not all sites accommodate a walkout style home. A walkout site has enough slope to expose part of the foundation and permit access to the yard from the lower level.

Possibilities the builder mentions could affect design, budget, schedule, or even all three. The builder can check on the development status to learn what types of services are available for the lot. Given sufficient time and motivation, anyone can find such answers, but a builder with an established network of contacts can obtain that information more efficiently.

Whether you decide to explore on your own, talk with friends and colleagues, or seek out other sources, do not rush this decision. You can remodel many details about your new home in later years as your lifestyle evolves, but changing its location is not one of them.

Driving Around

Tour the areas you marked on your map and look for land with "For Sale" signs. Note location, phone number, and enough descriptive detail to help you envision it later. A camera or camcorder can aid your memory. After several sites they all begin to blend together.

Real Estate Agents

Some real estate agents specialize in land sales. An agent can help you search for a lot and handle the paperwork when you make a final choice. Typically the commission on a land purchase is higher than that on a home purchase. If you have already decided on a builder, the commission is figured on only the lot sale, not the home. If the real estate agent helps you find a builder, a commission is due on the total package.

Real estate agents use the Multiple Listing Service (MLS) to learn about properties for sale. The MLS computer stores dozens of details about available lots. The agent inputs criteria such as size, price, or school system, and the system prints a list of sites that meet

Before showing you any home sites, the real estate agent should tell you whom he or she represents: the buyer (you) or the seller (land owner).

those needs. One disadvantage is that the MLS database does not include for-sale-by-owner sites.

Newspaper Ads

You can discover for-sale-by-owner lots in the classified ads of local newspapers. You may find some terrific sites this way, but remember that the newspaper prints what the person who placed the ad dictates. The screening process, an integral part of listing property with a real estate agent, does not apply here. As with all potential sites, investigate thoroughly.

Local Government

Most communities or counties today have a master plan or a comprehensive plan. The master plan defines the density of subdivisions, size of lots, and setbacks (how far from the edge of the lot to place the home). By reviewing this blueprint for growth, you can get an idea of what the future holds for the region. A planning board made up of citizens and guided by community goals oversees land use and the pace of development. The county planning commission or public library can supply information on zoning, the master plan, and maps.

Keep in mind that zoning is always subject to change. Real estate agents, builders, and subdivision sales staff can tell you what they know as of today. No one can guarantee that tomorrow someone won't organize a campaign to change the zoning—and your future view. A study of local newspapers tells you how steadfast the planning board is in adhering to the long-term community plan. However, history is only an indicator, not a guarantee. Circumstances, goals, and people in office can change in a short time.

Evaluating Potential Sites

Selecting your lot is as important as selecting your builder. You need to consider that, although you are the buyer today, you may someday become the seller.

If a site passed your preliminary screening, take a closer look. Go beyond casually walking around on the lot. Find the property pins at the corners of the property boundaries. If possible, visit the site at different times of day and in several types of weather. How would you position your home on the site? What about the sun, the view? Drive to and from work in both rush hours. Taking pictures can help you remember what is where, especially if you make your choice from among several sites.

Compare your lifestyle to the possibilities for the site. If your family enjoys morning coffee on the deck or outdoor activities such as gardening, volleyball, or children's games will this site adapt to those activities? What is the speed limit on the street, how much traffic passes or will pass the lot and at what hours? Will car headlights or street lights shine into bedroom windows? Make an effort to meet nearby neighbors. If you have young children, you may want to know if other children live nearby, as playmates or babysitters. If you are considering a subdivision site, which models, elevations, and colors would surround your home? Subdivisions usually open in phases. You may want to wait for the next phase to open to get your ideal lot (Figure 5.2).

**Figure 5.2
Imagine Looking
Out of Your House
at Your Lot**

Use the checklist in Figure 5.1 to evaluate and compare sites. Give yourself permission to change your mind during this process. You may find a lot with such a spectacular view that the 10 minutes it adds to your commute may seem acceptable after all. A few comments about some items listed in Figure 5.1 will make the checklist more useful to you.

Costs

Double-check all numbers, including any premium or unusual fees, to confirm that the price will not throw your budget into chaos. Exceptions are easy to find, but a traditional guideline is that the cost of the finished lot should run about 20 to 25 percent of the total package, house and land. (A finished lot includes streets and utility lines.) Property taxes, assessments, and home owners association fees can add a significant amount to your final cost. A large site may appeal to your sense of privacy—until you consider the cost of installing and maintaining a driveway.

Utilities. When comparing custom sites, check the status and cost of utility hook-ups or tap fees. If a lot owner has paid some of these costs, take that fact into account when comparing sites. If utility services are not yet available at the site, obtain information on the cost. Find out, too, how much time is needed for approval and installation of services. Water and sewer are critical issues. You cannot build a house without arranging for these services.

If public water and sewer service are unavailable, you will need a well and a septic system. Installing them involves several steps. Where your well is placed affects the cost and quality of the water supply. Wells are designated as either shallow (up to 50 feet) or deep. Properly constructed deep wells are more reliable and produce cleaner water. The cost of the well is determined by its depth. The required depth is only a guess until an adequate supply of water is reached.

The first step in installing a septic system is a percolation test or perc test, which measures the rate at which soil absorbs water. This rating determines the size of the septic system. The perc test also affects the distance needed between your well and the septic system. This distance ensures that water absorbed from the septic system does not contaminate the well. These locations will, in turn, affect the location of your house and can affect costs. Contact the local health department for specific details.

Impact Fees. An impact fee is a charge for the impact your new home and its occupants will have on infrastructure (roads and community services). These fees are significant in some parts of the country. Your house plan can carry impact fees of $0 when built on one site and $35,000 or more when built on another.

Premiums. Be realistic about view lots and the premiums charged for them. How likely is the view to remain intact? Once your home is built, if you can see the view only when you stand on the garage roof, you may regret paying the premium (Figure 5.3).

Home Owners Association

The term *covenant-protected* refers to the restrictions a home owners association places on the residents and homes in a community. A typical example of such a restriction is that neighbors cannot paint their homes purple with chartreuse shutters and a red polka-dot door. Of course, neither can you. Carefully review the documents of any home owners association for requirements and restrictions.

Some people believe that covenants are protective; others think they are intrusive. Whatever your opinion, recognize that associations do enforce covenants and that they usually win in court. Purchasing a covenant-protected site thinking you can ignore restrictions you do not like can end in a conflict you are likely to lose. Can your family live comfortably in a community that might enforce the following?

- a design review process in which a committee approves your house plans, architectural details, exterior materials, and colors
- controls on such items as recreational vehicles, fences, satellite dishes, swing sets, dog runs, and clotheslines

**Figure 5.3
A Premium View**

- fees for building or deposits to assure the site is kept clean
- approval required to remove trees
- limitations on operating a business from your home

Survey

As part of your site-selection process, you need to evaluate the site survey. Figure 5.4 explains some relevant terminology. Will the house you want fit on the lot? Is the lot appropriate for the style you have in mind? If you have not completed your house plans, you'll want to think carefully about the lot in making design decisions. Consider shape, size, angles, and massing of materials to blend your home design with a particular site. Will you be able to add to your home later? Your builder or architect can help you analyze the site and make these determinations.

Construction Factors

Physical conditions should support the design of the home, since the most appealing designs blend into their sites. Extensive grading, while physically possible, can get expensive. Within a subdivision, you may find potential grade changes limited by their effect on neighboring lots. Your builder or architect can help identify concerns, such as a slope too steep to allow a driveway, and offer suggestions to solve them. Other natural conditions to consider: wetlands, wildlife, rocks, groundwater, and trees.

Whether you build in a subdivision or on a custom lot in the country, listed below are some additional details you should remember:

- Even if you do not have children, remember that schools can affect resale value.
- Depending on traditions or local regulations, adjacent sites may drain across your property, and your property may in turn pass water along to another neighbor. Drainage swales do not always follow property lines, nor do they always respect your plans for a vegetable garden or play area for your children.
- Utility companies install junction boxes above ground. Neither you nor your builder can control where the utility companies place these boxes.

Figure 5.4 Lot Talk

The space the house takes up on the ground is its *footprint*. This footprint must fit within the *building envelope*, the space available for building after *setbacks* and *easements* are considered. Setbacks are the required distances from the edges of the lot or any easement. A 10-foot side setback means your home, shed, solar collector, or garage must be 10 feet or more from the sides of the lot. Setbacks are usually not the same for each edge of the lot. *Easements* are areas set aside for utility supply lines and other items to pass through the property. Easements allow service to your lot and adjacent lots now and in the future. Many lots include drainage easements, meaning runoff from adjacent lots passes across your property. Easements are recorded and are permanent.

- Similarly, the U.S. Postal Service dictates the style and location of the area's mailboxes. In subdivision communities, this situation often means a bank of centrally located mailboxes where residents stop to collect their mail.
- If having sidewalks is important to you, check on this detail before making a commitment.

Hazards

Every site may have some potential drawbacks, and a negative factor should not automatically eliminate a site from consideration. Be aware of possible extra costs and avoid surprises. Keep long-term goals in mind as well as today's needs. Many desirable areas come with natural hazards such as hurricanes, tornadoes, floods, or earthquakes.

On a smaller scale, think about winter driving conditions. Microclimate conditions, most often high winds, can affect a local area. Some regions post small-car warnings about strong wind around highways or signs that request that you limit your driving on "red" pollution days. Pollution can involve air, soil, water, or noise. You may find emissions from wood burning, traffic, agriculture, or factories annoying or even unhealthy; some of these emissions settle on the ground and become a permanent part of the soil. Nearby waste sites can affect the quality of well water. Nearby highways or airports sometimes bring sound pollution. Check into all these factors before selecting your site.

Lot Hold: Time to Think

A lot hold or lot reservation is useful when you need a little time to finalize your research or thinking. A lot hold should clearly document—

- complete names of the parties
- the lot held
- time frame of the hold
- amount of your deposit
- what happens to your deposit during this time (usually held without interest)
- that the deposit applies toward purchase if you decide to buy
- circumstances for return of your deposit (usually the expiration of the time period listed or your notice to cancel the hold)

Buying the Land

Except for the fact that land is impossible to move, buying land is like buying almost anything else. Once a lender has prequalified you, you're in a better position to make decisions about how much of your resources you want to commit to a land purchase. When you locate the lot you want, one option is to pay cash for it.

If paying the full amount in cash is not an option, you can finance the land. The same entities that offer loans for homes will typically offer loans for land purchase. Keep in mind that this loan creates a monthly liability on your financial statement that may affect your construction and mortgage loan qualification.

When purchasing a lot, use a written contract that specifies the location, includes a survey, and describes the exact terms of payment. You should have a title search conducted and purchase title insurance (see Chapter 11 for details on title insurance).

Once you've made the final decision, return to your choice of lender if needed, or get out your checkbook. You are about to become a land owner, and you are one step closer to building that new home.

Design, Specifications, and Budget

Your Mental Scrapbook of Housing Expectations

6

Home has a unique meaning for each of us. Throughout your life the homes you've lived in, visited, or read about contributed to your definition of a good house. This collection of ideas constitutes your mental scrapbook of housing expectations. To build the home that most closely matches the one in your scrapbook, make sure you're aware of what your scrapbook contains.

Lifestyle

People need space for interaction with others (dining rooms, great rooms, and media rooms); space for work (kitchens for food preparation, laundry rooms, workshops, and home offices); and space for privacy (bedrooms, bathrooms, dressing rooms, and walk-in closets). A sound design arranges the spaces in your home for effective use and then connects them with convenient traffic paths. Putting the kids' play area next to the home office may create sound problems, and few of us want to carry groceries through the living room to get them to the kitchen.

Analyze the needs of your family, as a group and as individuals. Should your plan include a home office, a study area, space for hobbies? Gourmets need counter space. Painters need good light. What needs do your family's activities dictate? Do you prefer formal or informal entertaining? Do you host out-of-town guests? If the kids have friends over for a video game marathon, where will you do those monthly reports? List what each family member does alone, and what you do as a group. Include holiday activities. Think about the present and the future. What changes do you expect in the next 5 to 10 years? Think about future needs, including such items as phone, cable, DSL lines, and electrical outlets.

Next, identify the details that change a house into a home for your family. Along with the practical factors, consider sights, sounds, even smells. The morning sunlight through the kitchen window, a distant train, or the fragrance of honeysuckle may define home for you. The right house for your family is one that rekindles the best memories while providing a setting for new ones.

Quality

Think about quality. Every builder claims to produce it, but your definition of quality is unlikely to exactly match anyone else's. For some, meticulous fit and finish signify quality. For others, features and function take precedence over aesthetics. Identify the specific characteristics you equate with quality. In making design decisions, consider not only aesthetics and function but maintenance needs and environmental impact.

Effect on the Environment

Materials and methods in new home construction are changing and improving every day. Efforts to use resources efficiently have led to the development of many alternative materials that take the place of wood in the home. Alternative materials offer choices that affect cost, the construction schedule, and long-term performance as well as the home's impact on the environment. Make the most of energy efficiency by planning for it from the beginning. Today's construction methods offer dozens of opportunities to reduce a home's energy needs.

Document Your Ideas

Turn your mental scrapbook into a form you can share with your production builder or custom design team. Assemble a literal scrapbook of sketches, photos, model numbers, samples, and color chips (Figure 6.1). Develop a page of notes and ideas for each room or area of the home. Review the list of New Home Selections in Figure 6.2 to start you thinking.

**Figure 6.1
Look at Other
Kitchens for Ideas**

Figure 6.2 New Home Selections

Exterior Elevation

- [ ] Colonial
- [ ] French Country
- [ ] Mediterranean
- [ ] Southwest
- [ ] Traditional
- [ ] Tudor

Entry

- [ ] Porch
- [ ] Foyer
- [ ] Entryway
- [ ] Single- or two-story
- [ ] Separate entrance[1]

Door

- [ ] Single or double
- [ ] Sidelights
- [ ] Transom
- [ ] All wood, metal, fiberglass
- [ ] Glass inserts
  - —Clear glass
  - —Etched glass
  - —Leaded glass

Stair Configuration

- [ ] Straight
- [ ] Curved
- [ ] T-shaped
- [ ] L-shaped
- [ ] U-shaped

Rooms

- [ ] Living room
- [ ] Great room
- [ ] Kitchen
- [ ] Nook
  - —Snack bar
  - —Pantry
  - —Kitchen desk
- [ ] Hearth room
- [ ] Formal dining room
- [ ] Family room
  - —Media prewire
  - —Fireplace or wood-burning stove
- [ ] Number of bedrooms
  - —Main floor master bedroom
  - —Master bedroom sitting area
- [ ] Number of bathrooms
  - —Closets
  - —Dressing rooms
- [ ] Library
- [ ] Den
- [ ] Home office
- [ ] Guest room
- [ ] Sunroom
- [ ] Laundry room
- [ ] Butler's pantry
- [ ] Mud room
- [ ] Utility room
- [ ] Garage
  - ___ 2- or 3-car
  - ___ Side entry
  - ___ Extra storage
  - ___ Workshop
- [ ] Basement

Design Details

- [ ] Ceilings
  - —Height
  - —Vaulted
  - —Coffered
  - —Flat
  - —Skylights
- [ ] Drywall finish
  - —Skim coat
  - —Texture
  - —Orange peel[2]
  - —Knock down[3]
  - —Southwest
  - —Rounded corners
- [ ] Wall finish
  - —Paint
  - —Wallpaper
  - —Wallpaper borders
- [ ] Interior trim
  - —Cased entryways
  - —Cased windows
  - —Crown molding
  - —Chair rail
  - —Picture panels
  - —Plate rail
  - —Built-ins
  - —Door style
- [ ] Electrical and lighting
  - —Ceiling
  - —Hanging
  - —Wall sconces
  - —Indirect
  - —Dimmers
  - —Security
  - —Decorative outlets
  - —Computer
  - —Fax line
  - —Internet access
  - —Freezer outlet
  - —Garage door opener outlet
  - —Integrated wiring
    - • Lights
    - • Security
    - • Temperature
    - • Ventilation
    - • Communication (intercom, phone, Internet)
    - • Entertainment
- [ ] Countertops
  - —Laminate
  - —Tile
  - —Marble or imitation marble
  - —Granite
  - —Concrete
  - —Solid surface (list brand)
  - —Edge detail
  - —Tile backsplash
- [ ] Cabinets
  - —Wood
  - —Laminate
  - —Knobs, handles, and drawer pulls
  - —Glass doors
  - —Shelf and rack inserts, roller shelves
  - —European (concealed) hinges
- [ ] Energy efficiency
  - —Solar factors
  - —High-efficiency furnace
  - —Extra insulation
  - —Foam core panels

---

1. For a home office, mother-in-law apartment, or quarters for a live-in maid/child care person.

2. An orange peel dry wall finish has the texture of a bumpy orange peel.

3. A knock-down finish begins as orange peel texture. The drywall finisher scrapes a long blade over the top to remove just the tops of the dots. It is popular in western states.

Setting Priorities

Your challenge is to build a home that matches your scrapbook as closely as possible. You want to duplicate the features you love, avoid those you dislike, and accomplish all this within your budget. Recognize that the items in your scrapbook arrived there without regard to cost. Now you need to prioritize the collection. In Chapter 2, prequalifying determined your total budget. Now you will work with your builder or design team to allocate that amount among the items that will become your new home.

Each decision for your new home influences cost and impacts other choices as well. How important is that three-car, side-entry garage? A side-entry garage requires a driveway that is shaped differently from the driveway for a front-entry garage, and that shape can affect the landscaping plan. Or would you rather apply the cost difference to granite and upgraded carpet?

Think of this process not as giving up things you want but as determining which items are essential and which are preferences. If you know from the beginning where the "must-haves" stop and the "would-like-to-haves" begin, choices become easier. If you must omit something, select an item you can add later, such as wallpaper, rather than sacrifice something that is impractical to add later, such as a curved staircase. Your builder can help you decide what is practical to add later and what is not. Keep resale value in mind, but keep it in perspective. Your family's needs and wants should come first. With your priorities clearly established, you are prepared to evaluate new design details, then accept or reject them.

Sources of Plans

By now you have organized your mental scrapbook on paper, perhaps with illustrations. Use these criteria as a guide to evaluate house plans. Jot down the pluses and minuses as you review floor plans. Note your reactions to exterior elevations, remembering to view all sides of each home. House plans are available for your review in a variety of formats.

Models

Probably the best way to get the full effect of a floor plan is by visiting the furnished models of production or semi-custom builders. Notice room size, layout, and traffic flow. Imagine your family's daily activities taking place in each home. Would the plan serve your family's lifestyle effectively and comfortably? Where would the kids do their homework? Where will you hang coats? Will the dining room hold your family for Thanksgiving dinner?

If you are exploring production or semi-custom homes, take special care to understand which features are standard. Review the builder's list of options. Standard options reflect the most-requested additions and alterations. The list should include prices, although these are subject to change. Ask about the builder's willingness to consider custom change orders and carefully review this wording in the sales agreement (see Chapter 4).

Study quality as you tour homes. Look carefully, then return to those you like and look again. Sit in each room, stand in every corner. Sit on the floor and look up. Listen to sounds that carry through the home. Have family members flush toilets, open and close doors, and

The quality you are looking at in the home you are touring is the quality the builder will deliver.

hold conversations as you move from room to room listening. Check how doors and windows fit, notice wood trim installation, and paint and stain coverage. Are drywall seams invisible and is the finish even? Examine materials, fit, and finish on the exterior.

Occupied Homes

Custom builders are less likely to have designated models. They can often arrange appointments for you to view an occupied home their companies built. Such visits provide you with a golden opportunity to see design and quality and speak with a veteran home owner at the same time. Ask what the owners like best about their floor plan and what they would change if they could.

Homes Under Construction

Builders who have model homes may not offer a sample of each floor plan but might let you tour homes under construction to experience a life-sized example. Although room sizes are more difficult to evaluate when a home is incomplete, seeing homes at frame, mechanical, insulation, and drywall stages offers an opportunity to see inside the builder's quality.

Blueprints: Homes on Paper or Computer

Selecting a floor plan from blueprints is considerably tougher. A home loses much of its personality when reduced to a two-dimensional drawing. Many people have difficulty visualizing spatial relationships and may feel overwhelmed looking at a blueprint. If possible, take the plans home to study. The symbols are just architectural shorthand and you can quickly learn the basics. Figure 6.3 shows some of the essentials. Most sets of plans include a key to the symbols used. Ask your builder or architect to explain any symbols you do not understand.

Plan Services. Plan services offer catalogs of house plans that you can study in the privacy of your own home. As with blueprints, you can take as much time as you want to study the plans. Illustrations provide additional insight into the personality of the plan. Consistent formatting means you can readily compare plans. Most plan services will make custom changes to their plans, but at a price. Some offer prepackaged variations that are available immediately. Figure 6.4 offers points to consider when selecting a plan service.

Computer-Aided Design. Production builders often use increasingly popular computer-aided design (CAD) systems, to develop their plans in-house. Semi-custom and custom builders might sit at the screen with you, the home buyer, to explore possibilities. Or the computer operator may input your floor plan requirements and allow the technology to identify plans that meet these criteria. CAD systems technology allows you to see changes to your plans in a few minutes or a few days instead of the few weeks often needed with hand-drawn plans. Depending on the software, both two- and three-dimensional viewings are possible. Changes are as easy as a few key strokes—adding a wall, moving windows, or changing room sizes. Alternatively, the designer incorporates changes from your last plan review meeting to produce revised drawings for the next meeting (Figure 6.5).

**Figure 6.3
Blueprint Symbols**

⊏⊃	Door bell or chime
⋈	Phone
⊖	Duplex outlet
TV	Cable TV outlet
$	Switch
$₃	Three-way switch
⟡	Light
⊏⟺⊐	Florescent light
⊖-S	Outlet with switch
⊙	Floor outlet
WH	Water heater
FURN	Furnace
⊠	Duct (end view)
S⏉A	Supply air
H⏉B	Hose bib
✳	Floor drain
Brick (plan view)
Wood wall (plan view)
Double-hung window in wood wall

	Sliding window in wood wall with brick veneer
2°	Swing door with size 2-foot door
3°	Bifold door
1R-2S	Closet rod and shelves (1 rod, 2 shelves)
	Detail elevation. Top letter designates which drawing; bottom number shows which page; arrow shows direction of view.
W8x15	Steel beam with beam type and size
⊖- - -	Steel column supporting steel beam
	Section view. Top number tells which drawing; bottom number is the page; arrow shows direction of view
9'-0" / 8'-0"	Ceiling pattern description with ceiling heights
12 / 6	Roof pitch shows rize in height (6") for every 12" horizontally.
R-15 / R-30	Insulation symbol is for walls and floors with R-values given.

Figure 6.4 Selecting a Plan Service

When considering a plan service, look for one that offers—

- plans drawn or reviewed by an architect or structural engineer
- specifications that meet the standards of a recognized national building code
- a procedure for custom changes or permission to make changes

- technical support for answers to construction questions
- alternate foundation designs
- the option of purchasing a master that you can use to make copies for trade contractors
- copyright release

Copyright

Are you aware that house plans are protected by copyright law just as the law protects books, music, computer programs, and other intellectual property? Creating appealing house plans requires design talent, knowledge, and a lot of hard work. House plans represent a significant amount of both time and money. Home buyers should understand that architectural drawings, blueprints, floor plans, and the like are more than just selling tools to builders—they are property.

Builders who work from a repertoire of designs are unlikely to provide complete sets of blueprints to buyers. They do not want another builder to benefit from their work at no cost. From an artistic standpoint, some designers want control over their creations and will not even sell their plans. Others may accept a royalty in exchange for permission to build their designs. You're likely to run into an obstacle if you ask the builder to make changes to another designer's original work. Under law, the only people who can make changes are the owner of the plans or someone to whom the owner gives a written copyright release. Make sure you build your home from plans you own or have the right to use. (For more information on copyright see David Crump's *Copyright Law for Home Builders.*)

Custom Design Team

Have you considered developing a one-of-a-kind plan? This choice is significant in terms of cost, time, and personal satisfaction. Development of plans for a custom home requires many meetings with your design team and what may feel like an overwhelming number of choices. Go back to your prioritized list of features for a good start on this process. Begin with the general size and shape of the home you want and work toward specific features.

Remember, you are not doing this alone. You might hire professionals from separate organizations or choose to work with a design/build firm. In addition to finding your ideal builder, you may engage the services of an architect, an interior designer, and a landscape architect. Finding one member of the team often leads to others through referrals and recommendations. An architect whose work you like may recommend a builder, or a builder whose quality meets your standards may suggest an architect, and so on. However you organize your design team, make good communication a top priority. Figure 6.6 suggests points to consider when selecting design team members.

**Figure 6.5
Computer-Aided
Design (CAD)
Graphic**

Using a CAD system to combine a photograph (background) of the view from a proposed home with a CAD-created image of that home (foreground) helps prospective buyers imagine living there.

Architect

The architect may remain actively involved throughout construction or may simply develop the plans and then serve as a consultant. If you wish to have the architect act as your agent during construction, your written agreements with the architect and builder should reflect this.

Figure 6.6 Selecting Design Team Professionals

When considering professionals to work with you in designing your home, keep the following suggestions in mind:

- Check with relatives, friends, and colleagues for recommendations.
- What are the firm's design specialties?
- Does the style and quality the designers are known for coincide with your needs and wants?
- Look at examples of their work.
- Ask to interview them and notice how well they listen.

- Are ideas they offer about your home clearly communicated, in line with your target cost, and relevant to your desires?
- What services do they offer?
- How do they charge? What's included? What's extra?
- Does their client load permit reasonable scheduling for you?
- Ask for and check references.
- Ask about formal training and professional memberships.
- Do they use computer-aided design (CAD)?

Interior Designer

Just as the details in your mental scrapbook were collected without regard to cost, neither did you require that they conform to a single style. If you are thinking that a nice mansard roof can pull together a southwest exterior and a Victorian interior, consider retaining an interior designer. Rely on this professional to coordinate design details, finishes, and color selections. This same designer can help you select window coverings and furnishings if you wish.

Landscape Architect

Although you should probably hold off buying that riding mower, you may want to begin discussing your landscape design. Decisions about the placement of your home on the lot, preservation of trees, and configuration of the drive and walks affect your landscape plan and its cost. If you're building in a covenant-protected community, make certain your landscape designer knows the association's requirements and approval process.

Custom Design Process

Meetings followed by more meetings. In between, the builder collects information for you and revises the working drawings. Each session brings you closer to your final home plans. Expect to look at floor plans, elevations, and samples. Study catalogs and visit showrooms. Be prepared to discuss interior trim and stairwell shape, appliances, cabinet styles, and countertops.

Some find this part of the process fun and exciting. Others see it as frustrating and confusing. It can cause arguments, laughter, worry, or joy—sometimes all in the same day. In a common scenario, buyers take weeks making up their minds about design details, then—still without having made the needed decision—call the designer or builder and ask why everything is taking so long. Accustomed to this question and the anxiety it represents, most designers and builders handle it with patience and humor.

Home Owners Association: Design Review Process

Each member of your design team must know all the design criteria your future home owners association uses in its design review procedures. Familiarize yourself with the design review committee's meeting dates so you can have any necessary approvals in time to start construction near the desired date. Keep the same concern in mind with regard to your landscaping plan. Read Figure 6.7 for more details.

How Much Will This Home Cost?

No one can tell you exactly what your home will cost until the design is complete. Many buyers find this ambiguity difficult to tolerate, but expecting an exact price at this point is like asking how much your dinner will cost before you have selected from the restaurant's menu. Throughout the design process, watch for items you want that you can withhold and add later after moving in if the total price exceeds the budget. A good design team can help you identify these details and point out many alternatives. Your builder can assist with

Figure 6.7 Design Review by the Home Owners Association

When a developer creates a covenant-protected community, a set of standards is identified for that community. The developer includes these standards in the Declaration of Covenants, Conditions, and Restrictions (CC&Rs) and files them with the county before the sale of any lot. Each lot is then sold with the understanding that the purchaser agrees to the CC&Rs.

You must understand the covenants that regulate design and construction when you build in such a community. A committee of the developer's representatives and some home owners, usually called the design review committee, reviews plans for new homes and exterior changes to existing homes. This review ensures a harmonious mix of designs and compliance with the standards set in the CC&Rs. Design review may affect house styles, colors, materials, sizes, landscaping, and landscape infrastructure.

Design review committees typically meet on a monthly basis. If your plans need changes to gain approval, you may find the start of construction delayed until after the next monthly meeting. This kind of delay can create havoc with your construction schedule. To prevent this situation from occurring, contact the design review committee early for information on their process and requirements.

a rough budget from the beginning, but the numbers change with each choice you make. The working budget is constantly fluctuating.

Put It in Writing

Keep written notes about decisions you make at each meeting with your builder or design team. The details of these meetings, which sometimes last several hours, become elusive as time passes. The number of meetings that occur is up to you. Some buyers need two, others are still making choices after eight or nine. The more detailed the specifications, the less room exists for interpretation and surprises. You can see an example of specifications in Figure 6.8. Note the level of detail shown. A full set is many pages long, and a well-written one allows apples-to-apples comparison of trade contractor prices. These specifications are part of your contract as described in Chapter 4.

Pricing the Home

Once you and your design team are comfortable with most details, the working drawings and specifications are finalized, and the builder begins the pricing process. The builder sends copies of your house plans and specifications to a list of potential trade contractors and requests pricing information.

Takeoffs, Proposals, and Estimates

Either the trade contractors and suppliers or the builder (sometimes both) prepares a materials list, called a takeoff. The takeoff lists the materials needed for each part of the job.

Figure 6.8 Sample from Interior Trim Specifications

Doors: Prehung, hollow core, hard board (tempered or untempered, steamed and pressed wood fibers), chateau pattern.

Base: LS-B211, finger joint (drywall corners are square).

Casing: LS-C211, finger joint, tack base only in vinyl areas.

Closet Shelf: Super shelf, as drawn, adjustable shelves wherever plan shows 5 shelves or adjustable shelves (using shelf standards and clips).[1]

- Linens will have fixed shelves.
- Shoe shelf in the master closet will be a tipped piece of particle board covered with T&G cedar closet lining; base will run right up to the bottom edge.

Shelf Cleats: Finger joint pine screen stock, 1×2 inch or 1×3 inch as needed.

Chair rail: LS-CR5, pine.

Crown: LS-22 with dentil molding, finger joint in living room and dining room.

- Oak in family room on fireplace mantle and at top of fireplace wall, see page 16 of plans.
- Octagon window in the bedroom extension over the garage will be a traditional wood unit; jamb will need to be extended because of the 5-inch (with drywall) wall thickness; octagon window will also need casing.

Exterior Doors: The front door will be a wood unit with sidelights. The jambs will be extended and the sidelight to door jambs will be covered with lattice.

Jambs: All closets include jamb and case; bifolds will have $\frac{3}{4} \times \frac{3}{4}$-inch pine wrap on the inside.

---

1. Super shelf is a pressed wood product 24 inches wide that is often used for shelving in closets. It can be cut in half to create a 12-inch wide shelf, then painted. Shelf standards are narrow metal pieces with slots every half inch that hold small metal shelf supports for adjustable shelves.

For example, a framing takeoff lists how many 2×4s, 2×6s, 4×8 sheets of plywood, and so on are needed to frame the home. Labor costs are calculated. This process is repeated for windows, interior trim, floor covering, cabinets, countertops. . . . You get the idea. Even calculated on a computer, this level of detail can take many hours. The trade contractors and suppliers return the plans, specifications, and a written proposal, or bid. Bids are good for a specified time, typically 30 to 90 days.

Precise bids are impossible for some categories. Trade contractors submit a time-and-materials price for work that includes unknown elements. Excavation is one example. On some sites, until the excavator begins digging, no one knows what conditions exist.

The soil test reveals only the composition of soil taken from the test hole. Conditions a few feet away may differ.

Selecting Trade Contractors and Suppliers

Builders typically request and review bids from more than one company for each category. Your builder's choice of trade contractors and suppliers should reflect quality of workmanship, availability, and price—not just price. A company that appears expensive may cost less in the long run by showing up on time and completing work efficiently and correctly the first time. For thoughts on using friends, family, or your own skills in building your home, review Figure 6.9.

Engineering

Where required, the builder selects an engineer who designs a foundation appropriate to the site and its soil conditions. If the site or the plan has unusual characteristics, the builder may ask for an opinion on feasibility early in the design process. The engineer may also do calculations to determine your home's structural needs. The structural elements are the parts that hold the weight of the home (known as dead load) and the occupants and their furniture (known as live load). Your home's size and configuration affect what goes inside its walls. In earthquake- or hurricane-prone areas, building codes impose special requirements to assure maximum resistance to damages. All these details affect the final cost.

The Budget

The semi-custom or custom builder develops the house budget as prices come in and incorporates in it the price from each selected supplier or trade contractor. The budget includes costs of permits, fees, taxes, insurance, and allowances as a contingency amount, usually 2 to 5 percent (Figure 6.10). The builder calculates and includes commissions for real estate agents, if applicable, and builder margin. These numbers lead to the first final

---

Figure 6.9 Sweat Equity, or Bring Your Own Bathtub (BYOB)

Many home buyers ask if they can supply materials or do installation work for some aspect of their home. Perhaps they are in a construction-related business or have a construction-related hobby. They hope to save money, have better quality at the same cost, have more choices, or enjoy the personal satisfaction of creating part of their own homes. This type of contribution is called sweat equity.

In exchange for savings in dollars, the buyer accepts certain types of risks and responsibilities. They initially include administrative chores and delivery responsibilities. The task grows from there to include scheduling, insurance, coordinating with other trades, and warranty of their own work. The liabilities for delaying other work, damaging work completed by previous trades, and failure to meet code requirements are also legitimate concerns.

Some builders do not work in this way, and those builders who do have learned to clarify the separate responsibilities from the beginning. While sweat equity situations offer potentially significant benefits, they also pose risks. To prevent problems, the buyer and builder should discuss the details thoroughly and put their agreement in writing before proceeding.

Figure 6.10 Sample Preliminary Construction Budget

A to Z Construction
1234 Main Street
Your Town, USA 56789-1234
(808) 555-9922

Walkout Ranch
3,255 Square Feet

Date _____
Mr. & Mrs. Home owner
(808) 999-8888

A. Fees, Insurance		**Subtotals**
1. Builders Risk Insurance	$ 780	
2. Permit	3,250	
3. Use Tax	4,160	
4. Well	12,350	
5. Septic	4,550	
		$25,090

B. Engineering and Surveying		
6. Structural	1,105	
7. Site Plan	455	
8. House Stake	163	
9. Improvement Survey	163	
10. Grading Certification	130	
11. Soil Report	520	
12. Footing Inspection	72	
13. Steel Inspection	72	
14. Drain Inspection	72	
15. H$_2$0 Proof Inspection	72	
16. House Plans	4,550	
		7,374

C. Utilities, Sanitation		
17. Power Usage	195	
18. Propane Tank & Fill	1,300	
19. Snow Removal	650	
20. Portable Toilet	663	
21. Trash Disposal	715	
		3,523

D. Excavation and Foundation		
22. Excavation	1,495	
23. Backfill	585	
24. Rough Grade	390	
25. Fine Grade	390	
26. Drive and Culvert	2,600	
27. Foundation	13,975	
28. Deck and Porch Caissons	663	
29. Waterproofing	345	
30. Perimeter Drain	1,170	
		21,633

E. Frame and Exterior Trim		
31. Frame Lumber	27,612	
32. Ext. Trim and Deck Mat.	9,620	
33. Trusses	8,931	
34. Beams and Posts	975	
35. Frame and Trim Labor	19,500	
36. Stairs	325	
		66,963

F. Mechanical		
37. Plumbing	11,050	
38. Heating, Ventilation, and Air-Conditioning	8,800	
39. Electric	6,656	
40. Light Fixtures	2,350	
41. Fireplace	1,495	
		30,381

First Column Subtotal		**$154,964**

G. Roofing, Gutter		
42. Roofing	17,225	
43. Gutter	1,105	
		18,330

H. Flatwork, Masonry		
44. Interior Flatwork	4,264	
45. Exterior Flatwork	3,120	
46. Precast Concrete Products	0	
47. Stonework	10,088	
		17,472

I. Insulation, Drywall, Paint		
48. Insulation	3,380	
49. Drywall	10,439	
50. Paint	7,904	
		21,723

J. Doors, Trim, Windows		
51. Entry Door	1,170	
52. Windows & Patio Doors	11,817	
53. Int. Trim Labor	3,453	
54. Int. Trim Material	5,012	
55. Hardware	1,060	
56. Garage Doors	1,729	
		24,241

K. Cabinets, Tops, Mirrors		
57. Cabinets	9,471	
58. Cabinet Installation	696	
59. Countertops and Installation	2,230	
60. Mirrors, Show Doors	1,105	
		13,502

L. Appliances, Floor Coverings		
61. Appliances	3,055	
62. Carpet	5,161	
63. Vinyl, Hardwood, Tile	5,707	
		13,923

M. Miscellaneous		
64. Equipment Rental	455	
65. Cleaning	1,060	
66. Landscaping and Tie Walls	2,080	
67. Mailbox	98	
		3,693

Second Column Subtotal		**$112,884**
Total Hard Costs		**$267,848**
Lot Cost	65,000	
Warranty Claims	2,009	
Contingency	4,017	
Subtotal		**$71,026**
Subtotal		**$338,874**
Profit and Overhead	59,800	
Total Costs		**$398,674**
Cost per Square Foot:	$122.48	

Note: This preliminary budget shows the categories that typically go into the price of a new home. Each decision can affect one or more categories. For example, if you select a coffered ceiling for the dining room, that decision will affect the cost of framing, drywall, interior trim, and paint. Additionally, this detailed work takes longer than a standard ceiling so construction loan interest increases slightly.

budget. The numbers contained in that first final budget can lead to some last-minute adjustments in design or specifications and result in a second final budget.

A well-done budget is detailed, comprehensive, and realistic. Construction lenders usually require this information as part of your application materials. While you may not receive a copy of the detailed budget, it is essential for the builder in managing the job. The lender checks invoices against this budget in the draw process (see Chapter 2).

The more customized your home, the more complex the pricing process becomes. Custom buyers must decide hundreds of details before their builders can finalize the price of a home. Production builders make most of these choices before offering their homes for sale. They offer a menu of prepriced options and may accept a few custom changes. At either extreme and in between, the buyers must make all available decisions before the builder can determine a final total.

Allowances

Although the builder must represent everything in the house budget to obtain construction financing, you may not have finalized all your selections. If so, near the end of the design process you and the builder may agree to use allowances as described in Chapter 4, Contracts and Agreements.

During visits to showrooms or when reviewing option lists, beware if you find yourself saying or thinking these words: "I've been thinking—we are going to live in this house a long time. I'm going to have what I want." Most home buyers spend 10 to 15 percent more than they originally intended because their mental scrapbook of housing ideas spins out of control. By setting priorities at the start, you can build the home you want and enjoy peace of mind on move-in day. A mortgage payment you can live with is an important feature to include in your scrapbook.

Preliminary Steps 7
"When Are They Going to Start the House?"

In many ways, building a new home is like becoming a parent. The decision represents a long-term commitment, costs a lot of money, and the results require care and attention from day one. Once you make the decision, you have to wait a while before the results show. Labor problems can affect either of the delivery dates, which are approximate in the early stages. At times you wonder why you made this choice; other times it feels like the best idea you ever had. Speaking as a person who has experienced both, having a baby is actually easier because it involves less bureaucracy.

When Will the House Be Done?

From the moment you decide to build, a natural question is, "When can we move in?" At this point the answer is a target at best. The builder cannot provide a firm delivery date because factors outside his or her control affect the time needed to build a new home. For example, delays in obtaining plan approval from the building department or your home owners association design review committee are not unusual, especially with a custom home.

Weather can delay excavation or laying the foundation. Weather concerns continue through framing, roofing, and exterior finish. Few products you purchase are assembled outdoors. As consumers we are unaccustomed to this vulnerability and its potential consequences. A shortage of skilled labor and delays in obtaining materials also affect schedules. Builders often wait for a particular trade contractor rather than employ an unfamiliar company. Any delay in finalizing your selections or requests for change orders can also add to the schedule.

Target Date

Your builder recognizes that timing is critical to planning your move. The initial target date will begin as just that—a target. Once the home is closed in, the builder can set a firmer date since weather delays are minimized. Rest assured the builder wants to close as much as you do. After all, when you get the house, the builder gets paid. Although a guaranteed date is unrealistic until closer to completion, the builder can provide regular updates. Understanding the construction process makes tolerating this ambiguity easier.

The Permit

Although a few areas have no permitting, inspections, or code requirements at all, most residential construction begins with obtaining a building permit. The process varies from simple to complex and can take a few minutes or months. It commonly involves several steps. The last one, filing the application for a permit, is fairly simple. You or the builder go to the building permit office and drop off a bundle of documents. Assembling this bundle, which comes from many different sources, is not simple. Fortunately, some of the documents already exist thanks to your preparations for the loan application.

Production builders handle all of this work for you. Large-volume builders assign an employee to obtain, or pull, permits. The builder's standard plans are preapproved, which simplifies the application process. At the other extreme, if you are building a custom home on your lot, you may actively participate in the process.

Applying for a Permit

Begin by visiting the building department to pick up a list of items required, an application form, and a list of the inspections and other criteria that must be met during construction. Figure 7.1 lists items typically needed but expect regional variations. Review all requirements before you begin assembling the materials.

One document may come from the water and sanitation district, another from the insulation trade contractor, another from the home owners association, and one from the truss company. Each jurisdiction has its own requirements and timetables. These requirements may seem arbitrary, but they result from health and safety standards that are becoming more sophisticated. The system is set up to ensure that your home is built in accordance with building codes that make your home a safe place to live.

Time Frame

Once you or your builder submit the application package, you both wait for the building department to approve it and issue a building permit. The amount of construction in the area directly affects how long this process takes. You may obtain the permit immediately or within a few days. If construction is active, obtaining the permit can take months. One

---

Figure 7.1 Items Typically Needed to Apply for a Building Permit

- Permit application form
- Site plan showing the house on the lot, the easements, and setbacks (2 copies)
- Complete set of plans (2 copies)
- Soil report (2 copies)
- Engineer-stamped set of foundation plans (2 copies)
- Engineered truss drawings (2 copies)
- Letter from water and sewer district

    —for a septic system, percolation test results
    —for a well, a well permit

- For a rural lot, a driveway permit to establish access to a county road, if applicable
- Letter of acceptance from the homeowners association, if applicable

summer my husband and I waited four weeks instead of the usual two for a permit to add a deck to our home. Extra work generated by applications for Fourth of July fireworks stands caused the delay.

Changes Required

Whether their review of your plans takes one day or one month, building department officials may require changes to the plans before granting approval. Such changes are neither optional nor negotiable. Building officials may note minor adjustments in red and approve the plans contingent upon those changes being incorporated. Major changes require plan revision and resubmission. Once the building department approves your plans, structural changes (changes involving load-bearing portions of the home) necessitate resubmission and another approval. Approval to change the structure can add weeks to the schedule.

Approval

Approval means you get a stamp on your blueprints and an inspection card with your permit number, similar to the one shown in Figure 7.2. While these items may not seem like much to show for the effort and money you've invested so far, they are evidence that someone besides you and your builder expects a new home to go up. Reaching this milestone is an exciting moment.

Cost

When you or the builder pick up the permit, you will need to pay the permit fees. The exact amounts vary, but these fees usually are not minor expenses. The total can include such items as those listed here and others that may apply in your area:

Permit Fee. This fee is usually based on the cost of the home, the size of the home (square feet or cubic feet), or some other criteria.

Plan Check Fee. Many building departments have specially trained plan checkers who check your plans, detail by detail, for compliance with applicable codes.

Tap Fees. Tap fees are charges for tapping into municipal water and sewer systems. In some regions these amounts are paid directly to the water and sanitation district.

Driveway or Street Cut Permit. To install a driveway or cut a space in an existing curb for your driveway, you or your builder may need a permit. If so, a fee applies.

Impact Fees, Use Tax, or Special District Fees. Your move impacts roads, law enforcement, fire protection, schools, and other community services. You support these services via impact fees, which can vary greatly by region and range from nothing to tens of thousands of dollars.

The Inspection Card

In most cases the builder keeps the approved plans (blueprint) and an inspection card or ticket on site during construction. The inspection card is the record of inspections performed by the building department. Figure 7.3 lists typical inspections; however, these inspections vary considerably among regions. Inspectors note the results of each inspection—approved or not approved—and sign the card. Besides being the official record, because the builder

Figure 7.2 Sample Combined Building Permit and Inspection Card

Any County, Any State
Building Permit and Inspection Card

48 HOURS BEFORE YOU DIG
CALL FOR THE BLUE STAKES

1-999-999-9999

FOR LOCATION OF UNDERGROUND
GAS, ELECTRIC, & TELEPHONE

CALL INSPECTOR WHEN READY FOR EACH INSPECTION

AGREEMENT

In consideration of the issuance of this permit, the undersigned hereby agrees to comply with all such laws and regulations in the location, construction, and erection of the proposed structure for which this permit is granted, and further agrees that **if the above said ordinances are not fully complied with** in the location, erection, and construction of the above described structure, **the permit may then be revoked** by notice from the county building inspector **and then and there it shall become null and void.**

ADDRESS __1234 Any Street__ PERMIT # __9999999__

OWNER __Amy & Harry Homeowner__ DATE ISSUED __2004__ EXPIRES __2005__

SETBACK: Front _150' ½_ Side _100'_ Side _100'_ Rear _100'_

BUILDING TYPE: OCC: ZONE: COMMENTS:

Building	Date	Inspector	Remarks or Corrections
•Steel - Footings/Caissons*			
•Steel - Foundation*			
•Yard Line Pressure			
•Frame (after rough electrical)	11-01-99	NR	OK
•Insulation			
•Dry Wall	11-30-99	BOT	App oh to Tape
•Final	2-28-00	BOT	Ok
Electrical	Date	Inspector	Remarks or Corrections
•Rough in before insulation & dry wall	10-26-99		
•Service			
•Final	2-25-00		OK Final
Plumbing	Date	Inspector	Remarks or Corrections
•Ground Plumbing**	8-2-99	WUM	Ok with improvement Survey
•Septic 1000 Tnk / 1000 Fld	10-14-99	TSR	OK
•Final	2-28-00	BOT	OK
Gas & Sheet Metal Work	Date	Inspector	Remarks or Corrections
•Vent			
•Duct			
•Inside Gas Line & Pressure	10-18-99	WUM	OK
•Final	2-28-00	BOT	OK
Final Approvals	Date	Inspector	
•Zoning Final			
•Fire Final			
•Health Department Final			
•Driveway	2-28-00	BOT	OK

*Engineer Letter Required **Improvement Survey Due

Call Inspector when you are ready for each of the above inspections.
CALL: (999) 999-8888 Anytown, Any State 12345
THIS CARD MUST BE POSTED AT THE ABOVE-STATED ADDRESS & BE
PLAINLY VISIBLE FROM THE STREET & AVAILABLE FOR INSPECT'S SIGNATURE

**Figure 7.3 Typical Building Department Inspections
for Residential Construction**

- Caissons or footings
- Foundation
- Rough framing
- Rough mechanical

    —electrical
    —plumbing
    —heating (and air conditioning, if
        applicable)

- Insulation

    —certificate from the insulation contrac-
        tor meets this requirement in most
        areas

- Drywall
- Final frame, drywall, electrical, plumbing,
    and heating, ventilation, air-conditioning

may not be on the site when the inspection is performed, the card is used to communicate to and inform the builder if the inspection was approved, or what corrections need to be made to have the construction approved. Once a house passes the rough inspections (framing, plumbing, and electrical), the builder can install drywall and then the bathroom and kitchen fixtures and appliances (Figure 7.4).

In some regions, if the inspection card is unavailable, the inspector will refuse to conduct the inspection. If this happens, the builder must request the inspection again and pay a reinspection fee. In other regions, few inspections are required and code enforcement is not so strict. Figure 7.5 describes the four building code organizations.

Building departments require that the builder return the completed inspection card at the end of construction to obtain a certificate of occupancy. Until the building department issues a certificate of occupancy, also called a "CO" or a "C of O," neither you nor your belongings can move into the home. Clearly, this inspection card is important.

Inspections

The same building department that issues the permit inspects the work as it progresses. Your builder knows approximately how much notice is needed to have an inspection performed. Many areas use a voice mail system for requesting inspections. The builder calls in and records the permit number, address, and the inspection needed. Inspections generally occur within a day or two of the request, but the capacity of building departments does have a limit. During busy times, building inspectors can get behind like anyone else.

Your builder must correct items the inspector notes. If subsequent work would conceal these items, construction may not continue until the corrections are complete and the home passes reinspection. The builder must then pay a reinspection fee. Reinspections are not unusual. Inspectors note a few items on nearly every home. The checks and balances of inspections add time and cost to the project, and they also protect the buyer and the builder.

Starting the House

Once the preliminary paperwork is done, your builder can get started with something that shows. In some jurisdictions, initial work can begin before the permit is issued. The build-

**Figure 7.4
Inspections
Preceded
Installation
of These
Merchandised
Bathroom Fixtures**

Figure 7.5 Building Codes

You can trace building codes back to Hammurabi in the 18th century B.C. In the years since then, codes have become quite complex. Since the early part of the last century, three model code organizations had existed in the United States. They provided education for inspectors and published code books. These nonprofit organizations developed the three separate sets of codes used throughout the United States:

- The Building Officials and Code Administrators International (BOCA), founded in 1915 focused its National Building Code on the northeastern and midwestern states.
- The International Conference of Building Officials (ICBO), formed in 1922 in the west, called its code the Uniform Building Code.
- From 1940 on, the Southern Building Code Congress International (SBCCI) served the southeastern states with the Standard Building Code.

A fourth organization, the Council of American Building Officials (CABO), served as an umbrella to coordinate the activities of the original three and foster consistency.

Members of these organizations include building and fire safety officials; government personnel; trade associations; and design, research, and construction professionals. Their tasks included establishing codes for exits, fire protection, structural design, sanitary facilities, light and ventilation, environmental controls, materials, and energy usage. Depending on where you were building, your home was influenced by one of the model codes developed by these organizations.

Although regional code development was effective and responsive to our country's needs, the time came for a single set of codes. In1994 BOCA, ICBO, and SBCCI established the International Code Council (ICC) as a nonprofit organization dedicated to developing the International Codes. The ICC published the International Plumbing Code in 1995, followed by the International Mechanical Code in 1996. By 2000, a complete family of International Codes, including the International Building Code, was available.

Most states now use the International Codes at either the state or local level. The benefits to you include improved safety and cost savings. These codes incorporate the lessons learned from past disasters to address fire, electrical, and structural safety for all occupants and access for people with disabilities.

As a practical matter, when different jurisdictions use the same model code, builders can use the same plans to build homes in two different towns, and thereby reduce expenses for plans, code books, training contractors, and so on. No matter which model code applies in an area, once a model code is adopted by a jurisdiction, it becomes law and builders must follow it.

ing department can explain how far work can proceed without violating any regulations. The first step is often as simple as removing trees, rocks, or debris. (For suggestions on preserving trees, review Figure 7.6 and see Figure 7.7.) The need for preliminary grading depends on the site topography, or surface shape. The builder may need to level the surface and rough out a drive. In other cases, staking the house can occur without removing or grading anything.

Figure 7.6 Preserving and Protecting Trees

Trees increase the value of a homesite, provide an appealing setting, and contribute to energy savings and comfort. Deciduous trees provide shade in summer and allow the sun to warm your home in winter. Evergreens provide color and a windbreak. Trees cleanse the air, buffer noise, and offer a home for wildlife; their roots prevent soil erosion.

In preparing the site for construction, you and your builder should carefully mark which trees to remove: trees growing where the home will sit and those that would interfere with access, gutters, or utility lines. Consider weather patterns, solar factors, and aesthetics. Thin dense areas so that remaining trees can thrive. Remove dead material for the sake of appearance and fire safety. Home owners associations may require approval of tree removal plans.

Protect trees you want to preserve from construction vehicle and foot traffic. Compaction of the surface soil harms root systems. Trees in an excavation area may show damage months later because of disturbance of the root system or changes in the drainage. With a bit of planning you can protect and preserve healthy trees and create a lovely setting for your new home.

Depending on your agreement with the builder, you may need to arrange for some of the site work such as drilling the well or installing the septic system. If so, take care to coordinate with the builder to keep progress running smoothly.

Staking Out the House

Working from the site plan, the builder or a surveyor stakes the location of the excavation. Stakes are 1×2-inch pieces of wood with colored ties. The surveyors pound them into the

Figure 7.7 Mature Trees Add Shade and Value

Photo by James F. Wilson, Dallas, Texas.

ground to mark the location of the home. Since the excavation area must exceed the size of the home to allow room to work, the excavator also needs another set of stakes. You can see an illustration of these stakes in Figure 7.8. The builder or surveyor installs this second set, called batter boards, a designated distance from each of the first stakes. The excavator then uses this second set of stakes as a guide to dig the foundation.

Safety

Everyone involved in building your home should keep safety in mind at all times. This is common sense, and to help make it more common, the Occupational Safety and Health Administration (OSHA) creates and enforces regulations for residential construction. Protective wear such as hard hats, gloves, and safety glasses; safety equipment such as harnesses or other fall protection for elevated work; and rails around stair holes are just a few examples of OSHA requirements. These efforts add to the cost of a home, but injuries are even more expensive and carry a high price in human terms as well. Resources are better used for prevention.

Home Owners Association Regulations

In addition to design review requirements, most home owners associations place restrictions on construction activities. For example, they may limit which roads construction vehicles can use, where parking is permitted, and the times of day work begins and ends. The builder provides appropriate trash containers and regular cleanup of the site. Your builder communicates these requirements to all employees and trades and should enforce them consistently. Home owners associations often require a deposit to assure compliance with their rules regarding construction activities.

**Figure 7.8
Staking the
Foundation**

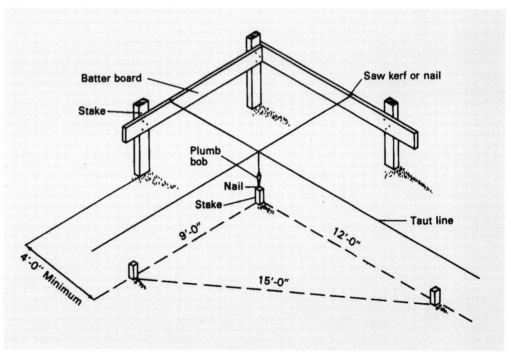

Reprinted from George E. Sherwood and Robert C. Stroh, eds. Wood Frame House Construction
(Washington, D.C.: Builder Books, National Association of Home Builders, 1988), p.17.

On-Site Working Conditions

Many jurisdictions require the builder to post the lot number and address on the site. Even if yours does not require this posting, it makes sense, especially for custom work. The installation of a trash dumpster and a toilet facility are signs that construction is about to begin. The builder orders temporary power for tools, equipment, and radios and may use a portable generator until the temporary service is installed. Some jurisdictions require gravel for a temporary drive; others require plastic mesh fences, called silt fences, to keep exposed soil from washing off the site. Hay bales can serve the same purpose. All these details cost money and are part of the house budget.

While all of this work is going on, your builder has also been signing contracts with trade contractors, planning a detailed construction schedule, preparing purchase orders, and answering any last-minute questions you may have, such as, "Is it too soon to pack?" Just when you think you cannot stand one more day of waiting, meetings, decisions, or budget revisions, you visit the site and see that some dirt has been moved.

Construction Process

"Is It Done Yet?"

8

Finally, the builder starts the house. By this time you are already well into planning furniture arrangements. Expect to second-guess some of your choices,
visit the site, get in some mud, worry about the weather, make some changes,
and wonder where all that money is going. You think everyone should hurry up and get
your home built. No, wait. . . . They should take their time and build it right. No, wait. . . .
The loan rate expires. The school year starts. The new job begins. Maybe they should just
take their time as fast as possible.

Depending on whom you talk to, you may dread a frustrating, stressful, expensive
nightmare, or you may look forward to a utopian experience with no glitches. Neither scenario is realistic. Delays, surprises, questions, dirt, noise, and more meetings and phone
calls than you imagined possible make up the building process. But expect fun and satisfaction too.

In the end, your impression of this experience as good or bad will depend on the
expectations you started with. Start with accurate and complete information, and you'll
have more realistic expectations for the construction schedule, jobsite protocol, your site
visits, changes, and quality.

Construction Schedules

The builder and trade contractors discuss the approximate schedule for your home. As
with the house budget, your builder creates a construction schedule based on experience
combined with input from the trades. Each trade contractor estimates the number of days
needed to complete its portion of the work. Production builders who build the same floor
plans repeatedly evolve a predictable schedule for each plan. Because custom and semi-
custom builders are usually using building plans that have not been built before, unantic-
ipated details that crop up can affect the schedule (Figure 8.1).

Sequence

Each trade contractor needs a certain number of days to complete its work, depending on
the size and complexity of the floor plan. Some portions of the work must occur in
sequence. For example, suppose you order rough-in plumbing for the basement. The
builder must have the sewer line for that future downstairs bath installed before the concrete basement floor is poured.

Figure 8.1
A Dream Home:
The Result of
Construction
Schedules Met

Photo by James F. Wilson, Dallas, Texas.

Some trades need to work alone in the house. Having the electrician and the plumber there simultaneously can result in frustration and inefficiency because they get in each other's way. However, some aspects of the work can overlap, especially later on, after the home is closed in. Interior and exterior crews usually do not interfere with each other's work, so the builder can run parallel schedules—one interior, one exterior. A carpenter can hang interior doors while the concrete contractor pours the driveway. Knowing which trades can work at the same time, from a practical and a personality standpoint, is part of your builder's job.

Critical Path

You may hear the term *critical path* used in connection with the construction schedule. This term refers to milestones in the building process that are critical to meeting the target delivery date. Between these milestones some variation in the order or exact timing of the work can occur. But if the work fails to meet one milestone, expect an adjustment in the final delivery date.

Schedule Formats

Builders format construction schedules in many ways. Some use a list, others bar charts. Still others have magnetic boards with moveable markers that represent each phase of the work. Many now use computers to track and update the schedule. Regardless of which method they use, construction schedules require regular revisions. And although everyone (not just you) would prefer to follow the original schedule and finish on time, these schedules seldom behave that way. A construction schedule is the epitome of a living document, and many factors can conspire to extend its life.

Lead Time

Once work begins, the builder should notify each trade several days or weeks before its assigned work date. Trade contractors need varying lengths of lead time, or notice, depending on how much construction is occurring in the region. The exact number of days varies with workload and from trade to trade.

The painter who needs three weeks lead time in June may need only three days in November. The electrician may need two days' notice, while the drywall crew needs two weeks. A month later, they all may need entirely different lead times. Staying in touch with these constantly changing workloads is part of the builder's job.

Material Delivery

Your builder also must time the ordering of materials so that deliveries occur at the correct time. If materials arrive too soon and just sit at the site, they risk damage or theft. If they arrive too late, someone ends up waiting for them. Suppliers need lead time just as trade contractors do. Again, the amount of work in the area affects this orchestration.

Final Selections

Speaking of schedules, your job at this point is to complete any design, color, or fixture decisions that remain. The builder must order many parts and materials in advance to have them on hand when needed. The sooner the materials can be ordered, the better, particularly if you selected custom items such as hand-painted tiles. If a product or color choice is no longer available, the earlier you know that, the more notice you have to select another one.

Construction Site Protocol

On the construction site, the builder is in charge of the trade contractors and you are in charge of the builder the same way you are in charge of a surgeon in the hospital. Although you are paying the bill, wisdom suggests you listen to your expert. After all, you selected this builder carefully. The relationship can include questions and debates and still remain successful for both of you.

Day-to-Day Activities

Your builder is involved with your home on a daily basis. This involvement includes monitoring and updating the schedule, talking with the trade contractors, and checking on deliveries. The builder also answers questions from tradespeople and resolves conflicting details. Sometimes the builder asks for comments from you to clarify details. When this request occurs, the builder needs your response quickly.

The hundreds of phone calls that go into building a home are an invisible component of the work. Voice mail systems, pagers, faxes, emails, and cellular phones make these communications more convenient, but they do little to mitigate the sometimes hectic nature of the process. Expect to find yourself on the phone a lot, especially if you are building a custom home. Unexpected trips to the site are common, as are daily episodes of faxing diagrams back and forth and visiting showrooms. Studying catalogs to make decisions becomes part of your daily routine. The process demands your energy, enthusiasm—and patience.

Expect your builder to frequently check the work at the site. The builder's reputation and your ultimate satisfaction with the product rely on this close attention. Technical standards such as building codes and specific requirements such as blueprints, specs, and change orders provide detailed criteria for these inspections.

Routine Paperwork

Each month, the builder reviews invoices for materials and labor, compares them to the budget, and approves them for payment. As part of this process, the builder completes the lender's draw forms. If a category exceeds the budgeted amount, the lender wants an explanation and documentation. Depending on the details of your contract and construction loan, you also may approve these bills. Certifications, inspection records, letters from engineers, and other documents accumulate as the home progresses, and the builder maintains these in the house file. That way, when time comes to obtain the certificate of occupancy, the required documents are readily available.

Your Site Visits

Few purchases in today's world offer us the opportunity to watch the manufacturing of a product. Building a home is unique in this regard, and that idea proves both exhilarating and frightening. The excitement of seeing your home progress is one reason you're building a home. But few of us know how many details were corrected in our VCRs, our vehicles, or our shoes before they arrived—pristine and ready to use—at the retailer. Mistakes will occur during construction. Good communication can prevent the anxiety you're likely to feel as necessary corrections take place in your home. Site visits fall into two broad categories: scheduled and random.

Before work on your home begins, talk with your builder about site visits and come to an understanding about them on such issues as frequency and procedures.

Scheduled Site Visits. Regular jobsite visits are popular both with buyers and builders. These visits offer you and the builder an opportunity to have each other's undivided attention. At agreed-upon points during construction, you meet at the site to review progress, discuss questions, and update the target delivery date. These visits might occur every week or two or upon completion of certain phases of work.

Random Site Visits. You may find the magnetism of your new home site irresistible, especially if you live close by. Scheduled meetings may not satisfy your desire to see what was accomplished today, your need to feel involved, or your concerns about quality. Your builder may set guidelines for days and times when your visits are welcome. Your safety, satisfaction, and the smooth flow of work are the prime concerns.

Safety

The builder may require that company personnel accompany you when you visit your home. Some companies ask that you stop at the sales center so they know you are on site. At various phases of construction, your builder may require you to wear a hard hat. While hardly flattering headgear, hard hats do help protect you. No matter who owns the lot, common-sense precautions always apply:

- Watch where you are walking. Electrical cords and temporary bracing are just two of many items that can trip you. Catching your foot in a newly cut hole for a heat vent hurts. Even the cleanest construction site can have a nail lying in wait for a human foot.
- Do not walk backward or gaze up while walking. If you want to gaze, stop moving. The tragic importance of this was dramatized by the death of the 11-year-old daughter of custom-home buyers. Her wrong step backward resulted in a fatal fall. Sites are recognizably safer today than when this incident occurred nearly 20 years ago, but the sobering image reinforces the need for caution.
- Stay clear of equipment that is making loud noises, emitting exhaust, lifting pallets of bricks or shingles, beeping, chugging, chortling, or belching. The folks operating such equipment may not see you and definitely do not hear you. In a competition for space, such equipment always wins.
- Pay attention to people working above you. Construction personnel working on the roof may not hear you arrive. Unaware that you are nearby, a worker may toss a scrap to the ground—only to have it land on you.

People Who Build Your Home

You meet many characters on the construction site. You might find reformed type-A executives who gave up corporate positions to create something with their hands. Later you might encounter proud craftsmen, rough laborers, and a rambler who follows the gyrations of the job market. Every job has at least one sharp-eyed curmudgeon and one eccentric philosopher—sometimes in the same person. Look for some rookies learning a new trade and a few youngsters working for next semester's tuition. This motley collection of skill and brawn builds your home. Their habits include smoking, chewing, and singing. Their attire and language reflect the hard work and outdoor environment.

Conversations range from stock market analysis to last night's game, from kids to hunting. Vehicles and spouses are compared between trading tools and passing materials. Sunday school manners have infiltrated few construction sites. If a hammer and a thumb come in close contact, a colorful description of that event is likely to ensue.

Overall you find a pragmatic group of people committed to doing a job. Woven through their efforts you should expect mud, trash, material scraps, lunch wrappers, gravel, more mud, blowing sand and dust, mystery parts, and vehicles of every shape and size. Depending on who's working, the musical repertoire ranges from country to rock to classical. Drugs, drinking alcohol, horseplay, and speeding vehicles are frowned upon by builders and can result in termination.

"Why Isn't Anyone Working?"

Despite the diversity of this cast of characters, from time to time they all seem to leave the stage simultaneously. At times nothing appears to be happening. If you visit the site Tuesday, then on Thursday and see no significant change, your home is in one of these lulls. You'll worry less if you understand the reasons for this inactivity.

Everyone Talks About the Weather. Depending on the area and the time of year, the builder may include weather days in the schedule. Until the home is closed in, precipitation and low temperatures can stop interior work. Exterior work is always subject to weather conditions. Concrete work and exterior staining or painting require certain temperatures. Postponing this work until conditions are right usually is less expensive than doing it twice.

High winds can also pose a problem. When weekend winds of 70 mph rearranged two corners of foundation forms, I canceled pouring the concrete. After the foundation crew corrected the effects of the wind, I rescheduled for the next day. That night more than two feet of snow fell—a good portion of it inside the foundation forms—and another postponement followed.

Pace of Work. Sometimes a trade completes its work ahead of schedule. Often the next trade has an assigned time your builder cannot change on short notice. On the other hand, despite the requested lead time, a trade may run behind schedule. Work the trade contractor is completing at another site sometimes takes longer than expected. Trade contractors do not always let the builder know about these delays. Many phone calls follow.

Based on past history or recent events, builders know which trades are difficult to schedule. A shortage of skilled labor for a particular trade, the time of year, and recent weather all can impact scheduling. For instance, if a hailstorm occurs, roofers are at a premium. Builders consider this fact in their planning. One late trade can force the rescheduling of several others. If that situation occurs, your home may lose its place in line with one of the affected trade contractors. That change causes another delay. The technical term for this is the *domino effect.*

When you feel impatient, remember that your builder wants the home completed as much as you do. Do your part to keep the home on schedule by making selections on time and handling changes effectively.

Inspection Days. At several points during construction, progress stops until the work up to that point passes required building department inspections. This normal pause occurs with almost every home. Further work usually must wait until the items noted by inspectors are corrected. Few homes go through construction without an inspector citing something. Lenders, warranty insurance companies, Federal Housing Administration (FHA), or Veterans Administration (VA) may inspect your home as well.

Deliveries. Materials the builder orders do not always arrive on time. Delivery of back-ordered or custom-made items is unpredictable. Even when materials are available, shipping and delivery can cause delays. Some shipments arrive on time but incomplete. Items may arrive damaged. The demand for construction materials for areas hard hit by natural disasters such as hurricanes can affect material supplies. The depletion of inventories ripples right through the system.

If these scheduling mishaps make you wonder how any home is ever completed, remember that your builder works with these circumstances every day. All existing homes were subject to the same factors. Just as the budget contains a contingency category for unexpected expenses, the construction schedule contains a few extra days to offset the effects of delays. However, even the extra days may not compensate for all the schedule extensions.

"Let's Move This Wall a Teeny Bit"

Although you invested considerable thought and time in selecting and designing your new home, some refinements may come to mind as you watch it take shape. Perhaps your financial circumstances change a bit and enable you to add something you originally omitted. Also many buyers find that visits to the site stimulate their imaginations.

For example, imagine you are standing on the subfloor of your new home, gazing at the view, smelling the lumber, listening to the hammers (or nail guns). A vision of an extended deck embeds itself in your brain. You can't concentrate at work. You can't sleep. Your appetite dwindles. It's time for a change order. But before you ask for a pad of them, review the effect change orders have on the construction process.

Production builders are more amenable than ever to accepting change orders, although their systems work most efficiently with minimal alterations. Changes have always been part of the process for semi-custom and custom builders. Changing your mind about an item in your home is okay, but the earlier you make those changes the better. Later changes may result in delays, confusion, or extra expense. For instance, some floor plan changes require structural engineering revisions. And that means resubmitting plans to the building department for approval. Repeating these two steps adds to the schedule and costs money.

Also, once parts are ordered and labor scheduled, a momentum builds that is difficult to stop or change. Late changes can cause errors because of conflicting information circulating among the people on site and among the trades.

Status of the Work

Just because an item is not yet installed does not mean that changing it is easy or inexpensive. You may awake one morning knowing that pickled oak cabinets were the wrong choice and cherry cabinets are right. Just because the oak cabinets are not in your home yet does not mean this change is free. Many suppliers charge a restocking fee for returning items to their inventory. While everyone waits for the new cabinet choice to arrive, the builder reschedules the finish work of several trades. For instance, the builder must wait to install countertops and sinks until the cabinets are set.

With enough time and money—your time and your money—your builder can change almost anything. If, as the exterior carpenters put the finishing touches on your Tudor style home, you decide that you really want a Colonial, you instantly become a construction legend. However, with enough of your time and money, even this change is possible.

Time for Research and Decision

When you consider making a change, you must endure the frustrating wait while information is gathered to help you make the decision. Pricing can take a few minutes or a few weeks. The builder must collect information from every trade affected by the change. As the buyer, naturally you want to know the cost and the effect on the delivery date before making a final decision. Meanwhile, work continues. Taking completed work apart also adds days and dollars. Sometimes it costs less to stop work until the decision is made rather than risk having to take work apart.

Cutoff Points

The earlier in the process you make any decision, the more time, money, and aggravation you save. If you are thinking of a change, discuss it immediately with your builder and get his or her assistance in making a decision. Your builder may provide cutoff points beyond which you agree not to request changes. Figure 8.2 is one example, although specifics vary greatly.

Figure 8.2 Cutoff Points for Changes

Guidelines such as these save unnecessary expense and avoid adding days to the construction schedule. Each builder has different cutoff points. Some builders have one deadline a specified number of days after signing the contract. Make sure you know your builder's cutoff points for changes.

Changes Affecting	Should Be Made Before
1. Foundation	1. Engineering and permit application
2. Windows, doors, and elevation	2. Foundation stage
3. Mechanical systems, cabinets, and appliances	3. Framing stage
4. Texture, wallpaper, hardware, and lighting	4. Mechanical rough-ins
5. Interior trim and floor coverings	5. Insulation stage
6. Landscape design and selection	6. Interior doors and trim

Change Order Form

Keeping these cautions in mind, expect to make some changes. Document each on a change order form such as the one in Figure 8.3. When signed by all parties to the original contract, this form amends the agreement. A well-written change order documents several important points.

Description of the Change. Be clear and complete in describing the specifics about the change, including model numbers, colors, or material specifications. Diagrams, a copy of a catalog page, or other information help prevent misunderstandings. Details left open to interpretation can lead to surprises. Clear communication in writing is vital, no detail is too small to mention if it matters to you.

Cost. The change order should itemize costs you incur for the change, the most obvious being material and labor. Credits for items deleted may offset some charges. Other possible costs include construction loan interest for days added to the schedule because of the change or the supplier's restocking fee.

Your builder may charge an administration fee or design deposit. This money pays for the extra staff time needed to revise paperwork, cancel the original instructions, and double-check to confirm that new choices are installed correctly. After you and the builder sign the change order, the builder must see to its correct implementation and is at risk for any errors.

Payment. The lender and the builder consider change orders an extra expense, like overages on allowance items. This cost was not included in the house budget nor in the construction loan, so can you expect to pay for a change order when you sign it (Figure 8.4). If your permanent loan amount allows for the higher total, you can have these amounts credited at closing.

Schedule Adjustment. Many builders show the schedule adjustment on the change order form. If more than one change order applies, the accumulated total of days can grow significantly. Occasionally, the number of days that multiple changes add to the schedule may overlap. Three changes adding 5, 3, and 4 days respectively may add fewer than 12 days to the total schedule if the work occurs simultaneously.

Figure 8.3 Change Order Form

Buyer _____   Date _____

Contract Dated _____   Plan _____

Street Address _____   Lot No. _____

City, State, Zip_____   Change Order No._____

Description of Change _____

_____

_____

_____

Drawing attached   _____

Delivery date adjustment   _____ days

Administrative fee $_____

Cost of change $_____

Construction interest $_____

Credit for deleted items $_____

Total $_____

Revised Schedule of Payments _____

_____

Purchasers have requested the change described above. By signing this Change Order, Purchasers agree to pay for the change(s) indicated and acknowledge that the estimated delivery date for the home is revised accordingly. This Change Order applies only when approved and signed by the Builder, and paid in full by the Purchasers.

Approved _____   Purchaser _____
              (Builder)
                                       Purchaser _____

Date _____   Date _____

Disclaimer. This sample contract is provided for educational purposes to illustrate the principles discussed in this book and should not be used as a form. The contract is designed to cover the major topics of consideration for most new residential construction contracts. However, the suggested contract provisions do not and cannot apply to every situation, nor do they comply with any particular state law. Some of the provisions will not apply to a particular situation, while in other cases, additional terms may be appropriate. Laws can vary, and some states may require specific language and formats for certain contracts. New home buyers should work with their builders and attorneys to prepare documents that meet their particular needs.

**Figure 8.4
Add a Fireplace
with a Signed,
Paid Change Order**

Photo by James F. Wilson, Dallas, Texas.

Caution: Put It in Writing. Most builders inform their trade contractors that changes from the plans or specifications must be in writing from the builder. This policy protects everyone; most importantly it protects you. At one company where this policy was not followed, the buyers talked the plumber into moving some water lines so they could center a large antique mirror over the powder room sink. This change of just a few inches created havoc when the cabinet order arrived. The cabinet fit the original plan, which showed the sink off center.

After untangling the confusion, the builder returned the cabinets, ordered the new configuration, and rescheduled several trades. The electrician had to return to relocate the electrical box for the light fixture, which the buyers had not thought of centering. They paid a substantial restocking charge to the cabinet company and an extra trip charge to the electrician. And their delivery date was delayed. The change order documentation system has evolved for good reason. Insist that everyone follow it—including yourself.

Quality

Many builders have developed formal (written) inspection procedures and schedules. Some builders tie their inspections to trade contractor invoice approval. Building inspectors, warranty insurance companies, FHA, VA, or your lender may also inspect the home. However, no one looks as closely as the person who is paying. No matter how strong the commitment of the builder and all the other inspectors, your commitment to the home's quality is the strongest, and your standards the highest.

No matter what the price of your home, you may reach a point where your standards for some aspect of the work exceed everyone else's. "Everyone" in this context includes building codes, industry standards, warranty standards, and your builder's standards. Also, you may not have the technical knowledge to judge the quality of every stage of the work. Trust and confidence in your building team are vital to your peace of mind at such times. Staying in touch with some inescapable realities may help maintain your comfort as well.

A Code Is a Code Is a Code

Building codes make no distinctions based on price. They require builders to construct all homes to the same level of safety and make no attempt to set standards for aesthetics. The same safety standards apply to electrical wiring in an $85,000 home as in a home costing 10 times as much. Separate sets of standards do not exist for level floors, plumb walls, insulation, or air conditioning.

Price, Size, and Features

Price differences are most obvious in size and features. Usually, the more expensive the home, the larger and more complex its design. A $597,000 home will have a longer list of features than a home costing $113,000. The more expensive home's master bath has a jetted tub with a brass faucet. Tile walls, including hand-painted accent tiles, surround the tub. Beside it is a spacious walk-in shower, enclosed by clear glass panels trimmed in gold-tone frames. The cabinets have raised panel doors with brass knobs and provide lots of storage space.

The master bath in the less-expensive home includes a fiberglass tub with a chrome faucet. Tile surrounds this tub also. The buyers select from eight colors, none of which include hand-painted accents. A shower rod comes standard, but space limitations prohibit a walk-in shower. A single cabinet beneath the vanity offers some storage space. Its unadorned doors have no hardware.

Although different in appearance and price, the plumbing in both tubs works without leaking. Neither tub has chips nor gouges. The tile in both baths meets the same standards. In time, grout and caulking in these two baths will need maintenance by the home owners. The cabinet doors all operate smoothly and are level. They all show variations in the way the wood took the stain.

Craft, Skill, and Pride

As detailed as codes are, many times during construction the builder and the buyers can exercise their discretion. They add attention to detail at a level that suits their personal taste and budgets. The level of performance in such decisions rests on experience, pride of workmanship, and that ever-present budget.

When a conflict arises between what a buyer wants and what that buyer can afford, the budget generally wins. Signing a contract with a builder whose price fits your budget, but whose standards do not meet your expectations, leads to frustration and conflict.

Building a home is part science, part art, and part plain hard work.

The buyers' best assurance that their new homes will meet their individual standards is a thorough study of the builder's other work. As one of the last handmade products available to us, each home is unique in the same way that an oil painting by a landscape artist is unique. The artist can stand in the same place and paint two versions of the same panorama using identical colors and canvas size. Yet in the end, each painting has a personality distinctly its own. Although you have viewed your builder's previous work, your "painting" will have its own personality.

Communicating Your Concerns

In most contracts with a builder, buyers agree to a noninterference clause. This clause means that you take questions or concerns to the builder rather than give instructions to trade contractors. Questions channeled through lines of communication your builder creates for this purpose will get answered.

Can the issue wait until the next routine conversation or should you contact your builder immediately? Buyers often have difficulty determining the urgency of their questions. No simple formula exists for deciding when you should mention a detail immediately and when it can wait until a routine meeting. Without a comprehensive understanding of the construction process, you may not know.

You should bring some details to the builder's attention immediately. For instance, if you order a pink bathtub and see a blue one delivered, your builder and the plumber will both appreciate your calling attention to the error. As much as you can, resist two temptations. Don't point out items the builder will come to in the normal sequence of construction. The day the framers start the first floor walls is not an appropriate time to mention that the house needs a roof. And second, don't call the builder excessively. Constant conversation, despite how much your builder enjoys chatting with you, prevents efficient progress on your home.

If you are in doubt about which category your concern fits into, play it safe and contact the salesperson or builder. In a product this complex, misunderstandings about specifications are possible. The appropriate course—working through the builder to resolve your concern—prevents further complications. Put serious questions or extensive lists in writing. Keep a copy and give a copy to the salesperson or builder. Everyone is busy and good intentions do not make good memories. Ask when to expect a response and note the date and with whom you spoke for your own follow-up.

Noted, Not Corrected. Your concern may involve a detail the builder already noticed or appreciates your pointing out. Still, correction may not occur immediately. The broken window you and the builder notice in February is replaced in April when the window company delivers the screens and performs final operation adjustments. Replacing the window right away is possible, but the additional costs of such extra visits add up and are unnecessary. Before your home is complete, it may suffer another broken window. If you believe your builder has omitted something you ordered, the first step is to get your paperwork out and confirm that the item is listed. Your builder will build your home according to what is in your signed documents—the contract, your selection form, and possibly change orders. If an item is included in these documents, you should receive it. If it is not in these documents, you chose not to order it or forgot to do so. However, remembering all these details can be confusing. If you find the builder has made a mistake, notify the company immediately. If you aren't sure, ask about the item to clear up the confusion and possibly avoid a delay in getting your home completed.

Early Stages Can Appear Wrong. If you believe your builder has omitted something you ordered, the first step is to get your paperwork out and confirm that the item is listed. Your builder will build your home according to what is in this file. If an item is included in the paperwork, you should receive it. If it is not in these documents, you chose not to order it. However, remembering all those details can be confusing.

If you find that the builder has made a mistake, notify the company immediately. If you aren't sure, ask about the item to clear up the confusion and possibly avoid a delay in getting the home completed.

Sometimes work may appear wrong when it simply is incomplete. Once you hear the explanation, you realize you are seeing an interim stage in a process that will produce exactly what you want. One buyer harassed the painter into staining trim darker and darker. With the final finish applied, the result was too dark. The buyer paid the cost of material and labor (carpenter and painter) to install new trim and finish it according to the builder's original instructions.

Variations in Material and Technique. Construction techniques vary from region to region. Even if you remain in the same area, new methods are developed daily. When you are familiar with one method, you would naturally question a different one. But that fact does not make the new method wrong. Listen to the explanation the builder provides with an open mind, and ask questions until you are comfortable. Home buyers who have always lived in Florida may question the Midwest builder whose homes do not include protection against hurricanes. My childhood home in Fairview Park, Ohio, had plaster walls and single-pane windows. If I built a home two blocks away from it today, the new home would include drywall and double-pane windows. The important point is to become familiar with the general sequence of steps in the construction process, keep an open and inquisitive mind, and above all enjoy watching your home as it takes shape.

Construction Sequence

Putting Your Dream in a Logical Order

9

Construction practices in Vermont differ from those in California. In Florida you see details that are inappropriate in Oregon. But building a home follows a logical order; the general sequence runs in a similar pattern. An overview of that sequence is provided here. To study any aspect of construction in more detail, refer to the reference list at the end of this book.

Foundation

Using the stakes as a guide, an excavator digs the foundation. As the diagram in Figure 9.1 shows, this area must exceed the size of the foundation to allow room to work around the foundation forms. The extra space is backfilled or filled back in later. Over time, this backfill area settles until the earth returns to its original compaction. Especially in areas with expansive soils, builders use care not to compact backfill soils too tightly to avoid lateral (sideways) pressure on the home's foundation.

Depending on the region, builders use concrete block, brick, poured concrete, or treated wood to create foundations. Common designs include slab on grade, crawl space, or basement. Some designs combine foundation styles, as in a home with a partial basement and a crawl space. Figure 9.2 diagrams a poured foundation and Figure 9.3 shows a block foundation.

Builders in areas with expansive soils occasionally use a structural wood floor in the basement. The builder begins with a 10-foot foundation wall, then attaches a wood floor approximately 2 feet up from the bottom. The resulting basement is the usual depth and includes an 18- to 24-inch crawl space under the floor. While expensive, this design allows the floor to tolerate soil movement better than a concrete slab.

The foundation stage is not as simple as it appears. For instance, in the case of poured concrete, the foundation crew places the reinforcing steel called for by the engineer's design. They set openings for windows, vents, beams, and utility connections. Along the top edge of the foundation they install anchor bolts, which framers use to secure the wall to the foundation.

Based on soil conditions, the engineer may require a perimeter drain. This drainage system runs around the foundation, either inside or outside the wall. Perforated pipe in a bed of gravel collects water and channels it to a sump pit or into the gravel beneath the

Figure 9.1
Excavation

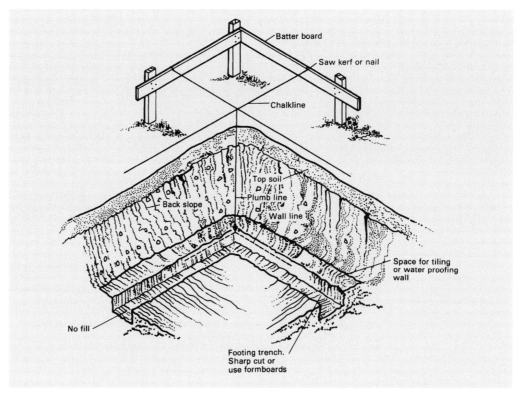

Reprinted from John A. Kilpatrick, Understanding House Construction, *2nd ed. (Washington, D.C.:*
Builder Books, National Association of Home Builders, 1993), p. 23.

Figure 9.2
Poured
Foundation

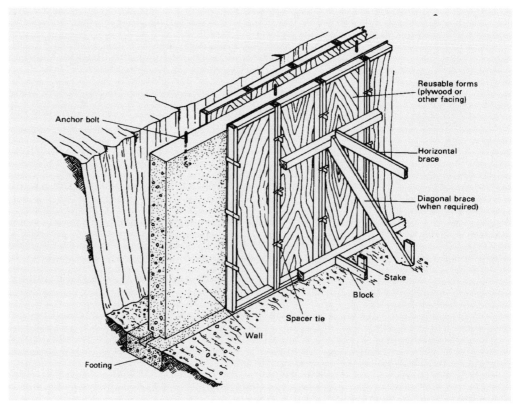

Reprinted from John A. Kilpatrick, Understanding House Construction, *2nd ed. (Washington, D.C.:*
Builder Books, National Association of Home Builders, 1993), p. 23.

**Figure 9.3
Concrete Block
Foundation
and Wall**

Photo by David Rhodes, Flagstaff, Arizona.

home's main sewer line. Installing a drain system during construction costs little compared to putting one in after the home is complete.

Before replacing backfill soils, the builder schedules waterproofing or dampproofing. This procedure involves applying an asphalt coating or sheet of polyethylene to seal the surface. If exterior foundation insulation is part of the design, it is installed at this point also. A foundation formed with polystyrene blocks serves two purposes. When filled with concrete, they form and insulate the foundation walls because the polystyrene remains in place. In jurisdictions that require foundation inspections, the builder contacts the building department to request that inspection.

Framing

If your plan includes a basement, framing begins with installation of the first level subfloor, followed promptly by the walls. Floor systems include joists of solid wood or engineered I-joists made of manufactured wood products or metal. The subfloor itself is often glued and screwed to the joists to minimize squeaks, although correct nailing can work as well. If your plan does not include a basement, framing begins directly on the slab.

As the photo in Figure 9.4 shows, dramatic progress occurs during the early stages at each floor level. Large expanses of walls go up quickly. Headers provide support across the tops of door and window openings or along the sides of holes for stairs. Beams provide support for floors. As these large components appear, the effects are quite noticeable. As the photo in Figure 9.5 shows, smaller interior wall sections, closets, and other framing details take a lot of time, but they do not provide the visual impact of installing the main walls.

Temporary bracing holds walls in place until the framers get all the pieces installed. You see permanent bracing, called sway bracing, on exterior corners. This reinforcement consists of 1×4-inch boards or metal straps installed diagonally, or a solid material such as plywood. This bracing holds the structure rigid and plumb. Some of the common elements of framing appear in Figure 9.6.

**Figure 9.4
Framing: Raising
the Wall**

The foreman of the framing crew and the builder regularly check how work is progressing. They look for correct size and placement of walls and door and window openings. They confirm that these openings are square. Rarely does a home go from foundation to completion without feeling the effect of some precipitation. The materials can withstand a considerable amount of weather. The builder watches for any effects that require correction. Even without precipitation, the builder closely checks framing. Our modern lumber supply is more unpredictable than in years past because current milling methods waste less of the tree.

Because of this concern and rising prices, manufactured wood products are increasingly important in home construction. Wood chips or veneers glued together form stable materials of varying shapes and sizes for construction use. Other products such as foam core panels, steel studs (Figure 9.7), air-entrained concrete block, and poured concrete homes are gaining in popularity.

Many roof designs today use engineered trusses for some or all of the roof support structure (Figure 9.8). (Trusses are preassembled hollow triangles or other shapes com-

**Figure 9.5
Interior Wall
Framing: A
Dramatic Stairway
with Safety Rails**

posed of wood or metal parts. These days trusses usually come factory-built. They are created in a controlled environment and delivered to the site ready to lift into place. A boom truck may do the lifting as the crew attaches each truss in its correct location. Some designs necessitate the framers building all or part of the roof skeleton on site. This stick-built method means the framers build the roof with individual pieces of lumber, sawed and nailed on the job.

Whether the roof is a truss roof, stick-built, or a combination, the framers install sheathing or decking next. Sheathing is solid material, usually plywood or a manufactured wood product. Roof decking consists of boards separated by small spaces to allow more ventilation. Your home's roof is a visible and practical application of geometry. With some-

**Figure 9.6
Common
Elements of
Framing**

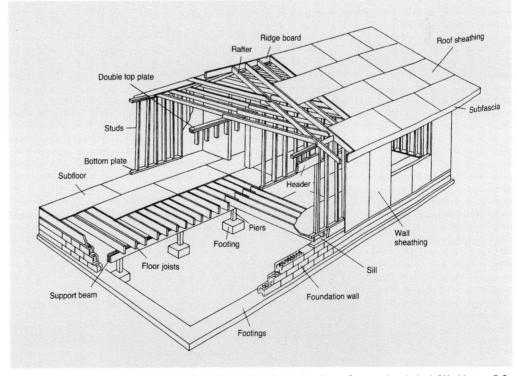

Reprinted from John A. Kilpatrick, Understanding House Construction, *2nd ed. (Washington, D.C.: Builder Books, National Association of Home Builders, 1993), p. 32.*

**Figure 9.7
Steel Framing**

Photo by NAHB Research Center, Upper Marlboro, Maryland.

times intricate combinations of angles and planes, the peaks and valleys of the roof then take on a solid appearance.

With sheathing complete, the plumbing, heating, and fireplace contractors cut holes through the roof. These holes accommodate the chimney and the vent pipes that exhaust the gaseous by-products of combustion and drains. Metal flashing and collars fit tightly around these chimneys, vents, and pipes. Caulking or tar seal the edges to make them watertight. The roof is now ready for the roofing contractor.

Roofing

Installation of roofing felt or paper begins at the lower edges and proceeds upward with each row overlapping the previous one. The roofer may also install flashing in the valleys, the angles where two planes of the roof slope down and come together.

Finally, based on the home's specifications, the roofers attach shingles made of asphalt, fiberglass, concrete, wood, tile, or slate. The variety of colors, textures, and shapes make this component of your home a significant design element. Today's roofing materials offer a wide range of choices, prices, and life expectancies.

**Figure 9.8
Trusses Set in
Place**

Exterior Trim

In some construction sequences, while the roofers install the roofing, the exterior trim crew begins their work installing fascia (boards nailed to the ends of rafters) and setting the windows and doors. Sheathing covers the framing and makes the walls of the home solid.

The finish materials go over the sheathing. Whether that material is siding, brick, stone, stucco, shingles, or a combination, once again progress appears rapid for a time and then slows as the workers begin to finish the details. You can see an example of the application of one form of stucco in Figure 9.9. The exterior trim crew installs details such as corner boards, door and window trim, columns, or shutters.

If your house plans include gutters, their installation can occur just before or after the roof goes on, although in some areas their installation occurs much later. The roofer may install these or your builder may hire a separate company that specializes in gutter work. Usually made of aluminum or vinyl, the gutters collect water as it runs off the roof and channel it to downspouts. A part of the gutter system, downspouts are the vertical pipes that take the roof runoff to the ground. This water should flow quickly away from your foundation. Splash blocks made of plastic or concrete or downspout extensions (a four-foot or longer piece of downspout) accomplish this task.

Rough-In of Mechanical Systems

The mechanical systems—heating, ventilation, and air-conditioning (HVAC); plumbing; and electrical—are each installed in two phases. Builders refer to the first phase as the

**Figure 9.9
Spraying
Three-Coat Stucco
on a House**

Reprinted with permission of Daniel Bang, Kenyon Plastering, Phoenix, Arizona.

rough or rough-in phase. In it, the mechanical subcontractors install parts you do not see when the home is complete. (See Figure 9.10 for examples of this work.) The ducts, pipes, and wires that circulate power, convenience, and comfort to various parts of your home are ultimately concealed inside the walls. Metal plates cover where a plumbing line passes through wood studs. The plates protect the water line from screws or nails during later work.

During this phase and according to your contract, the installation begins for the following systems, if applicable: intercom, security, in-wall vacuum, cable television, or in-wall entertainment. Extra phone lines, special outlets for computers, refrigerators, freezers, or garage door openers are most easily installed now. If you forgot one of these outlets, grab the nearest change order and fill it out.

Each mechanical trade returns later for the final phase of its work: installation of the fixtures, faucets, switches, and registers you see in the completed home. When rough mechanical work is complete, your builder calls for building department inspections on framing and rough mechanical work. Your home must pass all these inspections before anyone can start on insulation.

Insulation

Planning for energy efficiency makes sense for comfort, savings, and responsible energy use. Your choice of insulation may impact the energy efficiency of your house the most significantly. Minimum levels are strictly controlled by codes. Exceeding them is always possible and may mean savings in the long run.

Like the foundation design, the choice of what kind of insulation and how much is largely a matter of what is appropriate for the local conditions. In fact, the specific type can vary within the home itself, and both batt and blown insulation are common in homes. If your builder used foam core panels, the insulation is in those panels and so is already in place. Foam core panels look like ice cream sandwiches. They include two sheets of manufactured wood with polystyrene between them. They come in a variety of thicknesses.

**Figure 9.10
Electrical and
Plumbing
Rough-In**

Photo by David Rhodes, Flagstaff, Arizona.

Batts look like thick, narrow blankets and come in various thicknesses. Figure 9.11 shows the installation of batt insulation. Blown insulation is loose, so it can fill any specified depth, usually with the help of a large hose. This technique works well for places where installing batts is impractical, such as in an attic. Batts work well between studs. Most interior insulation today is made of cellulose or fiberglass, although variations are developing rapidly. Wet-spray cellulose, for example, is cellulose mixed with a small amount of adhesive, then sprayed onto a framed wall. When it dries, the excess is scraped from the faces of the studs. Batts made of cotton are also available.

Insulation is rated on "R-value," A measure of a material's resistance to heat flow. The higher the R-value, generally the better the insulation. The thickness and material the insulation is made from determine its rating. The insulation contractor certifies that the insulation meets the required R-values. However, small cracks can diminish the effectiveness of the most energy-efficient insulation. The insulation crews must carefully fill crevices around doors, windows, and vents. Disturbing insulation can also negate its effectiveness. For example, while storing boxes or connecting a speaker wire, a home owner might disturb blown insulation in an attic. Left uneven, this insulation no longer provides the original R-value.

Drywall

Because water damages drywall, the trade contractor waits until the roof is watertight to deliver, or stock, the drywall. In some regions, builders use two thicknesses (1/2-inch and 5/8-inch). Many building departments require the thicker material for walls shared by the home and garage. The thicker material provides greater fire protection. Drywall work proceeds in three main steps: hanging, taping, and finishing.

Hanging involves screwing or nailing the drywall into place. Using screws minimizes nail pops later. In some jurisdictions, the builder orders a building department inspection for this work. Next, a drywaller covers the seams with a thin tape and then coats the tape and screw heads with joint compound, referred to as mud. Several coats are required to accomplish this task with drying time in between. Finally, the selected texture is applied. If your decorating plans include wallpaper, leaving walls untextured saves a lot of work and mess later. Near the end of construction, a drywall patch person returns to touch-up the dings and dents that occur during completion of the home.

**Figure 9.11
Insulation Batts**

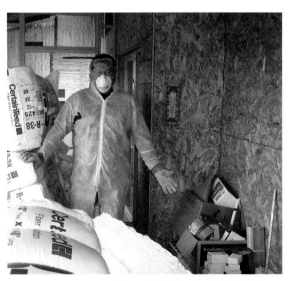

Photo by David Rhodes, Flagstaff, Arizona.

Interior Trim

The interior trim crew begins its work by setting doors. Most construction uses prehung doors that arrive with the jamb and door as a unit. Fitting this prehung door correctly into the rough opening assures a good fit and long-term performance. Baseboards and casings come next, followed by other interior trim called for in your plans and specifications. (Casings are the trim around doors and windows.) Crown mold, chair rail, fireplace mantel (see Figure 9.12), and the staircase (Figure 9.13) are examples of interior trim. The type of wood specified affects the amount of time this phase requires. For example, oak, which is harder than pine, takes more time to install.

Paint and Stain

The painter's responsibilities usually include sanding, filling nail holes, and caulking trim to drywall. Next, using sprayers, rollers, and old-fashioned brushes, the painter applies paints and stains as described in the specifications. Depending on colors and types of paint specified, painting sometimes involves several steps. The materials in the home are raw, so the first coat is a primer, followed by one or two finish coats. In a typical procedure, the painter applies enamel to the woodwork, then masks it off to spray the walls. The painter also expects to return later for touch-up work.

Finish Work

As the home enters the finish stage, the builder schedules cabinet installation (Figure 9.14), placement of countertops, and tile work (Figure 9.15). In comparatively rapid succession appear floor coverings, appliances, hardware, shower doors, mirrors, medicine cabinets, and screens. During this time, the mechanical trades each return to install fixtures and make final adjustments. These visits are called finals—final plumbing, final electrical, and so on.

**Figure 9.12
Interior Trim:
Fireplace Mantel**

**Figure 9.13
Interior Trim:
Stairway**

Reprinted with permission from Oakwood Homes, Denver, Colorado.

Meanwhile, outside, the painter completes painting or staining the exterior. Concrete or asphalt contractors install drives, porches, and walks. After the trade contractors remove any remaining debris from their work, the fine grader establishes the final drainage pattern. If your contract includes a sprinkler system and landscaping, that crew installs the sprinkler system, prepares the soil, and plants trees, shrubs, seed, or sod as called for in your specifications.

**Figure 9.14
Completed
Cabinet
Installation**

Reprinted with permission from Del Webb/Pulte, Lincoln, California.

Figure 9.15
Ceramic Tile
Installation

Reprinted with permission from Fred Parker Company, Inc., Fort Worth, Texas.

Construction Cleaning

Builders usually schedule two cleanings. The first, the construction clean, removes most of the dust and debris left by the work. Builders schedule window washing as near delivery as possible to minimize the possibility of time and weather negating the result.

Quality Control Inspection List

When the product created is so large that human beings carrying ladders walk around inside of it, dings and dents are likely. Every home contains patches and cosmetic repairs. The builder carefully inspects the home, noting the dings and dents and any details that need attention. The construction schedule includes days for work on this quality control list (formerly the punchlist). This list can result in a dozen trades coming back to perform last-minute tasks. Where required, the building department and other final inspections also occur now. Usually builders schedule a second cleaning, called the final or touch-up cleaning. Some builders wait to do this cleaning until after items discovered during the home buyer orientation are complete.

The builder also orders an improvement survey in preparation for closing. The surveyor provides a drawing that shows the property boundaries, the home, the drive, and other improvements. In most areas when construction is complete the builder presents the inspection records, survey, certifications, and probably some other documents to the building department. After one last review of these records, the building department issues a Certificate of Occupancy similar to the one shown in Figure 9.16. This important docu-

**Figure 9.16
Certificate of
Occupancy**

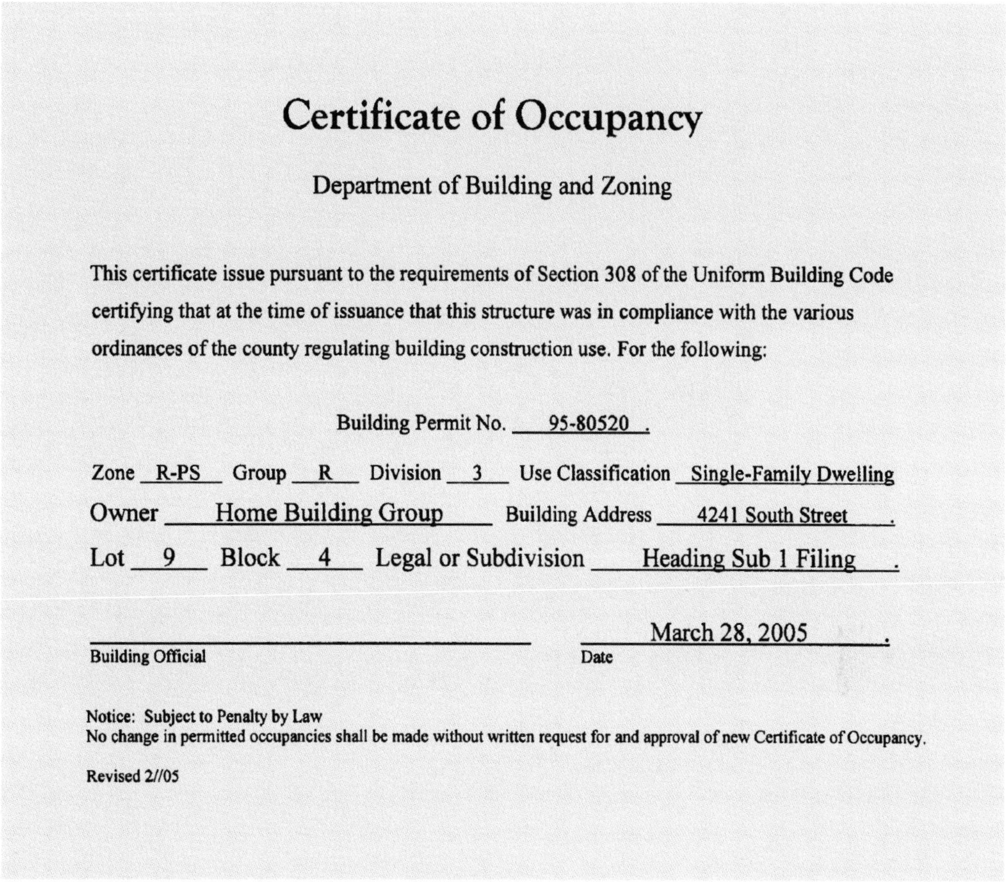

Certificate of Occupancy

Department of Building and Zoning

This certificate issue pursuant to the requirements of Section 308 of the Uniform Building Code certifying that at the time of issuance that this structure was in compliance with the various ordinances of the county regulating building construction use. For the following:

Building Permit No. ___95-80520___.

Zone __R-PS__ Group __R__ Division __3__ Use Classification __Single-Family Dwelling__

Owner _____Home Building Group_____ Building Address ____4241 South Street____.

Lot __9__ Block __4__ Legal or Subdivision ____Heading Sub 1 Filing___.

_____   _____March 28, 2005_____.
Building Official   Date

Notice: Subject to Penalty by Law
No change in permitted occupancies shall be made without written request for and approval of new Certificate of Occupancy.

Revised 2//05

ment, often called the "CO" or "C of O," means that at last you and the builder may close on the home.

Before closing occurs, however, your builder provides you with an orientation—your best opportunity to learn about your new home. During this orientation, you and the builder also confirm that the details you contracted for are correct. The next chapter discusses this process in detail and explains how to get the most from it.

Home Owner Orientation

"I'm Not Picky, But . . ."

10

As settlement approaches, tension mounts—along with exhaustion, change orders, questions, and excitement. Dozens of details compete for your attention: *Will the builder finish the house on time? Does the loan lock expire on the 27th or 28th? The view off the deck is just wonderful. Can the builder get the chipped kitchen sink replaced? Will the fine grader make a flat area for the vegetable garden? The paint on the shutters is not the color we picked, I don't care what the designer says. Fortunately, it looks terrific. The carpet color is perfect, but we need a new couch. We can't have this old thing in the new living room. Did I call the gas company yet? Where is that roll of packing paper that was just here?*

Introduction to Your New Home

In the middle of the barrage of detail and emotion, your builder schedules your home owner orientation. A home owner orientation goes beyond the traditional walkthrough. In the past, this meeting was mainly an inspection of the home. Now it is also a thorough demonstration of your new home.

Builders realize that demonstrating the home and providing information about its care benefits everyone. Not only are the new owners more comfortable, but this meeting can minimize calls to the builder's office. Home owners who understand the new day–night thermostat do not need to call the builder when they want the furnace to come on.

The orientation can also prevent problems. You are unlikely to self-clean the chrome trim rings from the range after learning they turn purple from the high temperature of the cleaning cycle. This kind of practical information saves you aggravation and expense.

Confirming Details

Besides demonstration and education, the orientation provides an opportunity for you to inspect the home. The builder, the building department, and your lender all checked the home. That may seem like a lot, but no one looks at a new home the way the people who live in it do. As with other aspects of home construction, builders use a wide variety of procedures to manage this process. Chances are your builder will discuss these with you before the actual meeting.

Scheduling Orientation

Expect several days' notice for the orientation appointment. Some builders set a tentative date weeks in advance. If your schedule demands more notice rather than less, make your builder aware of this situation. Allow at least two hours for the orientation. Most take 90 minutes, others up to four hours. That may seem like a long time, but a house is a big product with many parts to demonstrate and check. Avoid scheduling your orientation over a lunch hour or on a day when other appointments compete for your attention.

Aside from not rushing, another factor to consider when making the orientation appointment is lighting. Avoid late afternoon appointments. Dramatic streams of sunlight, harsh shadows, or even a setting sun can make it difficult for you to see surfaces clearly. Generally builders offer appointments Monday through Friday, from 8 a.m. until 3 p.m. A few offer Saturday morning appointments.

Ideally the builder conducts the orientation several days before the closing appointment. This allows the builder time to complete any noted items before you move in. If a serious issue arises, you and your builder have time to resolve it and still close on time. On the other hand, having three weeks between the orientation and closing needlessly increases construction loan costs, an expense ultimately passed on to home buyers.

Preparation

To take full advantage of your orientation, you need to do some preparation. During these last days, keep in mind that you and your family have experienced what many describe as an emotional roller coaster. Patience is running thin at the same time that anticipation is peaking. Plus, everyone is just plain tired. Tired of keeping appointments, making decisions, and digesting important information. And you're tired of change orders, schedules, and budgets. No matter how pleasant your lenders have been, you're probably tired of them, too. Certainly you're tired of signing checks. Your usually diplomatic self may have disappeared. Keep a good sense of humor, or at least a sense of balance.

Do Your Homework

If you haven't already done so, read the builder's limited warranty, warranty standards, and the literature on home maintenance. You should have received this information when you signed the contract. If you did not, or if you packed it with Aunt Matilda's lace tablecloth, ask for a copy. Make note of questions to ask.

Bring Your File

Plan to bring your contract, selection sheets, and change orders to the orientation. This orientation is the appropriate time to check each change order and confirm it was completed. If any questions come up about choices or colors, having the documents on hand helps.

Preview Orientation Forms

Ask for and read copies of the forms the builder uses for the orientation. If your builder supplied a home owner's manual, you may find copies there. Orientation forms document your acceptance of the home subject to correction of items noted. An example of one such form can be seen in Figure 10.1. Formats vary from a page of blank lines to elaborate checklists several pages long. The builder should note any items the two of you agree need further attention even if the work is already pending.

Enjoyable But Still Business

Experience shows home orientations are most beneficial when buyers can focus on their home and the information their builder presents. Arrange for friends to visit a bit later. If possible, bring young children out to see the home before or after the orientation. A bored youngster can distract you from your main purposes: to learn about your new home and to inspect it. If a real estate agent participated in your transaction, he or she is usually welcome but is not required to attend.

Orientation Fashion

Wear comfortable clothing and shoes that are convenient to get off and on. Avoid wearing a new navy blue suit as one home buyer did. His builder's procedures included having a painter present to do touch-ups immediately. The buyer pointed out a couple of spots and later leaned on the fresh paint. Paint or no paint, you will bend over tubs, kneel in front of the fireplace, walk the property boundaries, and so on.

Good clothes are a handicap at an orientation.

Participate

Arrive for your orientation rested and alert. Plan to listen carefully. Much of what the builder explains is in writing somewhere in the manufacturer's literature you are about to collect. However, you may not want to sit down and read that material as soon as you get your house keys. You should make a point of doing so soon; these booklets contain good information. For now, though, pay close attention and take notes.

A hands-on approach helps you remember the dozens of details your builder mentions. Touch the reset button on the disposal. Set the dishwasher and turn it on (remove any literature or sample detergents first). Try the sink sprayer. Open and close cupboards, drawers, closets, doors, and windows (Figure 10.2). Test smoke alarms, flip breakers, and handle your furnace filter.

Procedures

A few builders ask the buyers to go to the sales office at the appointment time, but most meet the buyers at their new homes. Depending on the structure of the company, the superintendent, assistant superintendent, warranty manager, or a customer service person whose full-time job is conducting orientations might conduct this meeting.

Itineraries

Builders follow a set route through the home for two reasons. First, to assure everyone that nothing is missed, either in the demonstration or the inspection. Second, noted items are easier for service personnel to find if the route through each home is essentially the same.

Figure 10.1 Orientation Inspection Form

Date _____ Lot No. _____

Purchaser(s) _____

Street Address _____ City, State, Zip _____

Phone_____ Cell Phone _____ Email _____

We believe that your home is complete, in satisfactory condition, and meets the quality standards described in your contract documents. We invite your confirmation of this fact by offering you an opportunity to review your home at this time. Your signature indicates that with the exception of items noted on page 2, the components listed below are in good and acceptable condition, including, where applicable, the cosmetic surfaces of these items. Cosmetic damages noted subsequent to those identified today and listed on page 2 are excluded from warranty coverage except as specifically described in your home owner manual.

Cosmetic Surfaces in Acceptable Condition

☐ Appliances
☐ Brass fixtures
☐ Cabinets
☐ Carpet
☐ Caulking
☐ Ceramic tile, grout (walls, counters, floors)
☐ Countertops
☐ Decks and exterior rails
☐ Doors
☐ Drywall
☐ Fireplace doors
☐ Garage overhead doors
☐ Hardware (knobs, towel bars)
☐ Hardwood floors
☐ Landscaping (sod, shrubs, trees)
☐ Light fixtures
☐ Granite, marble, or manufactured marble, and solid surface material
☐ Masonry
☐ Mirrors and medicine cabinets
☐ Paint
☐ Plumbing fixtures (sinks, tubs, faucets)
☐ Resilient floor coverings
☐ Shower or tub enclosure
☐ Siding
☐ Stairs and railing
☐ Stucco
☐ Windows, screens, patio doors
☐ Wood trim

Selections and Change Orders

☐ All selections and change order items are installed

Status Summary

(*Where appropriate, circle the correct answer.*)
☐ Grade: Complete Pending
☐ Air-conditioner: Charged Pending NA
☐ Crawl space: Dry Damp NA
☐ Smoke detectors respond to test buttons.
☐ GFCIs respond to test-reset buttons.
☐ Outside faucets function without leaks.

Manufacturers' Literature and Parts Delivered

☐ Heating system
☐ Air-conditioning
☐ Humidifier
☐ Water heater
☐ Range
☐ Broiler pan
☐ Cooktop
☐ Range hood
☐ Microwave
☐ Dishwasher
☐ Disposer
☐ Disposer wrench
☐ Sink strainer and drain cover
☐ Fireplace
☐ Garage door openers or keys
☐ Paint and stain samples

Warranty Service

For your protection and to allow efficient operation of our services, our warranty system is based on your written list of items. Please refer to Section 8 of your _[Builder's Name]_ Home Owner Manual for complete details.

Figure 10.1 Orientation Inspection Form (*Continued*)

Date _____ Lot No. _____

Purchaser(s) _____

Street Address _____ City, State, Zip _____

Inspection Items	Company Use

Home owner_____ Builder _____

All items listed above have been resolved.

Home owner_____ Builder _____

Date _____ Date _____

**Figure 10.2
Check How
Appliances,
Drawers, Doors,
Systems, and
Other Items Work**

The floor reflects the
overhead track
lighting.

As anxious as you are to measure for drapes or begin planning your workbench, stay with the builder to avoid missing useful information.

Agenda

Whatever the itinerary, as you proceed, the builder pauses many times to demonstrate or discuss the home's components, benefits, and features. Some companies have lists of as many as 180 items to talk about during the orientation. Such agendas are preplanned, practiced, and supported with information from manufacturers and feedback from other home owners. Figure 10.3 shows a portion of one such agenda. Though you may desperately want to discuss the dining room chandelier, listen to the information about grading and drainage and hold your questions until the tour goes inside. A wise practice is to come to the orientation with notes to remind you of any questions you want to ask. You are less likely to forget them in the excitement of touring your new house.

The builder usually presents information about each area, describes its benefits, and demonstrates its features. He or she also describes what to expect from your home as time passes and what services come with limited warranty coverage. Before moving on to the next area, everyone looks for details that do not meet the company's standards or comply with the contract.

Materials Delivered

At the orientation, the builder provides a list of emergency phone numbers in case you need assistance from critical trade contractors (electrical, plumbing, heating) outside of normal business hours. Some companies put this information on a sticker you can apply inside a cabinet door near the phone. Make sure manufacturer warranties and booklets are at the home: appliances, furnace, air-conditioner, and so on. If any are missing, the builder should note that on your orientation list and obtain copies for you.

The orientation is a good time for the builder to pass along recent updates on products or the community. This season's pool hours, the latest news from the cable television

Figure 10.3 Portion of an Orientation Agenda

Kitchen

- Self-cleaning range

  —Explain steps to operate.
  —Caution about chemical oven cleaners.
  —Caution about self-cleaning top of broiler pan, trim rings.
  —Confirm broiler pan is included.
  —Point out hood filter, discuss cleaning or replacing.

- Sink

  —Run water, check that water heater is on, check temperature.
  —Point out water shutoffs under sink.
  —Check for leaks.
  —Check sprayer.
  —Demonstrate how to clean aerator.

- Disposal

  —Run briefly.
  —Point out reset button.
  —Discuss importance of running cold water while operating.

- Dishwasher

  —Confirm that racks and basket are in good condition.
  —Discuss various settings, energy-saving features.
  —Point out rinse-aid dispenser.
  —Operate dishwasher, confirm that water is on.
  —Mention temporary new appliance odor.

company, or an announcement regarding the new community recycling program are examples. More and more builders provide a new home touch-up kit. The typical kit includes small cans of the paints used, a tube of caulk, and several small tools.

Important Paperwork

The forms you previewed provide you and the builder with a record of the home's condition at the time of delivery. The builder should give you copies of all pages used. At the end of the orientation you and the builder sign one or more of these forms to acknowledge that cosmetic surfaces and breakable items in your home are in proper condition. Note any exception on your orientation list.

Your builder's limited warranty does not provide repairs for damage caused by moving in or living in the home. If your movers scratch the marble entry floor bringing the piano in, you will discuss that with the moving company. If you splinter some wood trim and break a taillight backing out of the new garage, neither your builder nor your dealer owe you repairs.

Builders make common-sense exceptions, such as repairing damage a builder employee or trade contractor causes while working on an orientation item. However, these examples are clear-cut; and the responsibility for repair is obvious.

Conflict arises with less clear-cut events when no one is certain who caused the damage. The scratch on the kitchen counter that you noticed four days after closing might have been caused by the builder, the movers, a family member, or your wallpaper installer. You believe you missed seeing it at your orientation and ask the builder to replace the countertop. The builder believes someone in your household damaged the counter and refuses. What follows this conversation is not fun. Avoid a hassle and look carefully at breakable items and cosmetic surfaces such as those listed in the sample shown in Figure 10.1.

Preinspection

If you visit your home a day or two before orientation you may feel your calm demeanor slipping away as you consider how long it would take you, working with your own two hands, to attend to the details you see. Expect some last-minute rush; after all, if the home were complete, you would already live in it. Much of the fine-tuning that polishes a home for delivery must wait until final installations are complete. The builder's Quality Control Checklist can contain 100 to 200 items or more.

At orientation you should find that your builder has completed many of the items you saw in your preinspection. The builder can have several employees and trade contractors working on the home in those last few days. Each person brings different skills to the home. They may also bring in some dust that the touch-up cleaning staff should whisk away before your arrival for orientation.

As with so many aspects of new home construction, many approaches to orientation can work well; do what is comfortable for you.

Depending on philosophy, experience, and schedule, some buyers want to make a room-by-room list of their own at this point. Use a checklist if this approach appeals to you. Your list may duplicate the builder's efforts, but your peace of mind is worth it. Other buyers prefer to let all this activity occur in their absence and check the results at orientation.

Hired Inspectors

Some buyers hire a home inspector to check for compliance with building codes. Building codes set standards that address health and safety issues, leaving aesthetic matters for others. A professional inspector provides one more set of eyes to check your home's compliance with codes. Because they cost $300 to $450 or more, you'll want well-trained eyes. Select your home inspector carefully and have realistic expectations for the outcome. The inspector should—

- belong to the American Society of Home Inspectors
- know the codes that apply to your jurisdiction
- have experience with new home construction methods
- view your home as close to the day of your orientation as possible (Some inspectors do two inspections, one just before drywall and one shortly before orientation. Two inspections can cost up to twice as much as one.)
- provide an itemized report of any problems noted

Supply your builder with a copy and suggest discussing the items after the builder has had an opportunity to review the report.

What Do We List?

Items listed are those you and the builder agree need further attention. Typical categories are listed in Figure 10.4. If you mention an item you believe needs more attention, the

Figure 10.4 Categories of Orientation Items

Orientation items fall into several categories including

- incomplete or missing (cabinet knobs not installed)
- incorrect (porch light should be polished brass, not antique)

- dysfunctional (bath fan does not come on)
- below company standard (mitered corner not smooth at top right of den door, hallway side)
- damaged (scrape on wall from carpet installation)
- uncleaned (mud on garage floor)

builder will review it. If something does not meet the builder's promised standards or fails to meet contract specifications, the builder notes it and arranges for additional work. Most builders examine the home with you and volunteer items that are not up to their standards, even if you are unaware of them. The builder's name is on this home, too. The best builders notice something they could improve in each visit to the home.

Expect to note a reasonable number of minor items. This advice leads to the questions, "What is reasonable?" and "What is minor?" Reasonable and minor are matters for your judgment. A typical list contains 5 to 30 items. The real issue is, are you comfortable? Some general perspectives may help you decide.

Items Pending

Some work may be in progress; any builder can reach the orientation appointment with a few items pending. Unless the builder expects to have the work completed before you leave at the end of the orientation, the item should appear on your orientation form. Intentions are usually good, but memories are faulty.

Parts and Pieces

The contract, blueprints, specifications, selection sheets, and change orders delineate the products and materials for your home as well as installation and finishing techniques. The same paperwork establishes the possibility of substitutions and slight variations. Check that all the designated parts and pieces are present, correctly assembled, and in working order.

Surprises

No matter how meticulously you and your builder documented details, items you did not discuss may arise. Last-minute questions might sound like these: The deck isn't sealed? Plastic window-well covers do not come with the house? Only one towel ring in the powder room? The documents of your purchase, the models, and standard practice in the region provide criteria for resolving these questions. The builder may always use discretion and go beyond normal practice to satisfy a customer when misunderstandings occur.

Quality

Models or perhaps occupied homes created by your builder provide samples of the quality you can expect. At some point, quality is no longer scientific; it's a matter of personal taste. Every home has a subjective side and in a few matters your personal tastes may exceed the standards of the highest-quality builder. Legends are created by buyers who sit on the floor stroking the baseboard behind the toilet in the master bath to search for imperfections in the wood trim.

Attempts to change the builder's quality standards this late produces frustration or conflict rather than satisfactory results.

Any home, at any price, by any builder has items that could have been better. The question is: Did the builder achieve the overall level of quality shown in the model or described in the documents of the sale (Figure 10.5)? Did you get what you paid for?

Major Problems

Rarely does a major concern turn up during orientation. Serious items are usually noticed well in advance. For example, an almond range was installed when you ordered a white one, the garage door is the wrong style, or the patio is 2 feet short. Based on how the builder has been to work with up to this point, you must make a choice that comes down to this: assume the worst case, that the builder does nothing more on your home. Can you live with the condition, correct it yourself, or pay for work needed? You must choose between the risk and the inconvenience of postponing the closing until the matter is resolved. This matter rests on your individual judgment and a test of your trust in your builder.

Finishing Touches

Unless your orientation occurs at 11 a.m., closing at 1 p.m., and move-in at 3 p.m., your builder should make noticeable progress on remaining items before your move-in. The benefit of a few days between orientation and closing are clear. Builders who operate on that schedule may set a second appointment the day of closing to confirm completion of items noted during the orientation.

If a part is needed or a particular trade contractor must return, completing the work may take extra time. The builder should keep you informed of the expected scheduling for remaining items. Ten business days is reasonable, although 30 days is not unheard of (thanks to the service revolution, though, 30 days is heard of less and less).

Builders today are more likely to ask to have an adult present while any work is performed in your home.

Arranging access to occupied homes to complete orientation items is a concern for home owners and builders alike. Fewer builders accept keys after the home owners move in. On the other hand, making appointments around your busy schedule may mean service takes longer than anyone wants. This situation is one of those rock-and-hard-place issues. Builder and trade contractor service hours are typically 7 a.m. to 4 p.m., or 8 a.m. to 5 p.m., Monday through Friday. Saturday appointments are becoming more common but are still not the norm because supervision, suppliers, and the usual support systems are unavailable.

**Figure 10.5
Judge Your
Builder's Quality
by the Models and
Your Documents
of Sale**

Reprinted with permission from Doris A. Pearlman, MIRM, Possibilities for Design, Denver, Colorado.

All these concerns demonstrate why it's smart to have several days between the orientation and the closing. In the meanwhile, use the checklist in Figure 10.6 to keep track of items you may have overlooked during the home owner orientation. While the builder is attending the last-minute details on the home, you are attending to the last-minute details for your move. All the thinking, planning, deciding, paying, and waiting are about to give way to carrying, unpacking, arranging, and yes, more paying. But first, some paperwork called closing.

Figure 10.6 Home Owner Orientation Checklist

Exterior

- [ ] Elevation
- [ ] House numbers
- [ ] Property boundaries
- [ ] Water meter and street shut off valve
- [ ] Electric meter and main shut off switch
- [ ] Gas meter and main shut off valve
- [ ] Telephone connection
- [ ] Cable TV and high-speed computer connection
- [ ] Final grade complete
- [ ] Outside faucets
- [ ] Sprinkler system
- [ ] Deck/patio
- [ ] Gutters and downspouts
- [ ] Window weep holes
- [ ] Outside lights
- [ ] Exterior outlets
- [ ] Paint or stain
- [ ] Caulking
- [ ] Shingles
- [ ] Siding or stucco
- [ ] Masonry
- [ ] Chimney
- [ ] Trim and shutters
- [ ] Exterior doors
- [ ] Concrete slabs
- [ ] Outside lights

Entry

- [ ] Doorbell
- [ ] Walls and ceiling
- [ ] Floor and trim
- [ ] Floor covering

- [ ] Entry light
- [ ] Front door
- [ ] Locks
- [ ] Threshold
- [ ] Electrical outlets
- [ ] Register

Hall

- [ ] Walls and ceiling
- [ ] Floor and trim
- [ ] Window and screen
- [ ] Attic cover
- [ ] Electrical outlets
- [ ] Linen closet, shelves, door
- [ ] Register

Bedrooms

- [ ] Walls and ceiling
- [ ] Floor and trim
- [ ] Doors and doorstops
- [ ] Windows and screens
- [ ] Register
- [ ] Closets, shelves, and rods
- [ ] Light
- [ ] Electrical outlets

Bathrooms

- [ ] Walls and ceiling
- [ ] Floor and trim
- [ ] Door, doorstop, and privacy lock
- [ ] Window and screen
- [ ] Sink and faucet
- [ ] Stopper
- [ ] Toilet
- [ ] Tub/Spa
- [ ] Shower
- [ ] Shut off valves

- [ ] Tile
- [ ] Countertop
- [ ] Cabinets
- [ ] Mirrors
- [ ] Medicine cabinet
- [ ] Light
- [ ] Fan
- [ ] Caulk and grout
- [ ] Ground Fault Circuit Interrupter (GFCI) Outlet(s)
- [ ] Register

Attic Access

Stairs and Rail

Thermostat

Living Room

- [ ] Walls and ceiling
- [ ] Floor and trim
- [ ] Windows and screens
- [ ] Switched outlet
- [ ] Register

Dining Room

- [ ] Walls and ceiling
- [ ] Floor and trim
- [ ] Windows and screens
- [ ] Chandelier
- [ ] Electrical outlets
- [ ] Register

Family Room

- [ ] Walls and ceiling
- [ ] Floor and trim
- [ ] Windows and screens
- [ ] Fireplace
- [ ] Electrical outlets
- [ ] Register

Garage/Basement

- [ ] Breaker panel
- [ ] Overhead door
- [ ] Opener
- [ ] Garage floor
- [ ] Window
- [ ] Furnace and air-conditioner
- [ ] Water heater
- [ ] Electrical outlets

Laundry Room

- [ ] Water heater
- [ ] Walls and ceiling
- [ ] Floor and trim
- [ ] Window and screen
- [ ] Light fixture
- [ ] Shelves or cabinets
- [ ] Electrical and hose connections and dryer vent
- [ ] Other electrical outlets
- [ ] Register

Kitchen and Breakfast Nook

- [ ] Walls and ceiling
- [ ] Floor and trim
- [ ] Windows, screen or patio door
- [ ] Range/cooktop and oven
- [ ] Range hood
- [ ] Sink
- [ ] Disposer
- [ ] Dishwasher
- [ ] Countertop
- [ ] Cabinets
- [ ] Floor covering
- [ ] Register

Closing

"I Need HOW MUCH?"

11

A lso called settlement or close of escrow, closing involves a lot of paper and a lot of money. When it all stops sliding back and forth across the table, you own your new home. Congratulations!

Celebration aside for the moment, the ultimate purpose of the original sales agreement is finally achieved at closing: ownership of your new home is transferred from the builder to you. The technical steps include finalizing your loan (one set of papers and checks) and the builder selling you the home (another set of papers and checks). Next the money is disbursed to the appropriate people and companies including real estate agents, attorneys, title company, and surveyor, just to list a few. The builder transfers the title of your house to you, and the lender records your loan against your new property.

This process sounds easy enough, but it involves about 75 documents and almost as many checks. Some of the documents are duplicates, but you need to sign nearly all of them. Depending on how many questions you have, closing should take from 45 to 90 minutes. To understand how you achieve closing, you need to review the process one step at a time.

Settlement Agent

Depending on where you are building, your lender, a title company, an attorney, a real estate broker, or an escrow company can serve as the settlement agent and orchestrate the closing. The settlement agent's services include such details as ordering the title work and property survey and organizing all the paperwork for the closing itself. Chances are either your builder or your lender has experience with closing agents in the area and can suggest several. Carefully compare the services provided and fees charged before making a final choice.

Closing Appointment

Expect several days' notice for the closing appointment. Practices vary widely as to who sets up this appointment: your salesperson, a closing coordinator, someone from the title company, or your lender. Whoever sets the time should confirm the location with you. Closings can take place at the title company's, the lender's, the attorney's, or the real estate agent's office—actually any place that has a large table and lots of pens.

Escrow Closing

In some parts of the country an escrow agent handles closing. An escrow agreement specifies that the buyer and the seller each deposit required documents and funds with the escrow agent within a set time frame. Assuming the buyer and seller live up to their obligations, the escrow agent shuffles all the papers, records the necessary items, and gives each party its share of the money and the paper. The closing takes place in steps. At some point you sign all the papers and deliver all the money. One or more days later, the escrow agent records the transaction. Once recorded, the escrow is closed. You own your home and can pick up your keys.

Preparation

Whether you close in escrow or in person, preparation is the key to preventing last-minute panic or unexpected delays. Several details require your attention. You can handle most of these by phone, but problems arise if you wait until the last minute. By addressing these details during the weeks before closing instead of the days before, you have time to calmly resolve any last-minute glitches.

Insurance

You need to obtain and present proof of a home owner's policy from your insurance company. The actual policy is not required, just a certificate confirming coverage. Your insurance agent will have a standardized form for this. Arrange for this coverage no later than three weeks before the expected closing date.

This insurance policy should also list your lender as an insured. Check with your loan officer ahead of time for the company's complete legal name and have your lender's name and phone number handy for your insurance agent. Your agent may also ask the location of the nearest fire hydrant, the home's construction style, and price.

Utilities

Avoid surprises and frustration by contacting all applicable utility companies a few weeks before your move. The goal is to have your service begin as close to the closing date as possible. The utility companies may shut service off if the builder's name is removed from the account without yours taking its place. Make no assumptions about the availability of telephone service and do not rely on the experience of your new neighbors. Workloads change and lead times fluctuate. Call early to avoid inconvenience. The cable TV company may not provide service to a new area until a predetermined number of homes are occupied.

Unresolved Issues

The closing table is only for closing. Your builder may attend but is not required to do so. The same applies to your lender. Closing agents are not authorized to negotiate or make representations on behalf of any party at the closing. Therefore, if any issues remain unresolved, you are not ready to close. Finalize all negotiations, conversations, arrangements, agreements, adjustments, and deals before going to closing so you can relax and enjoy the barrage of papers.

Lender Conditions or Contingencies

Your loan approval may have included one or more contingencies that you must satisfy.

Find out exactly what is needed to satisfy contingencies and bring those items to closing.

Addressing each contingency completely ahead of time avoids any last-minute crises. For example, if closing the sale on a previous residence was a condition of loan approval, you need copies of those closing documents to close on your new home. Your statement, "We closed on the old place last Tuesday," will not suffice. The closing agent will nod patiently and ask again to see the documents.

The Final Number

Your final number is the amount of money you must bring to closing in order to leave with house keys. Some of the items included in the total, such as property tax and interest on your new loan, are subject to proration. These numbers change depending on whether you close on the 17th or the 25th. Therefore the closing agent cannot calculate the total until you have a definite closing date. If the date changes, even by one day, the agent recalculates the total based on the new date.

Form of Payment

Depending on local tradition or your lender's requirements, you may need to bring cash or certified funds to closing. Don't forget to allow time to obtain these funds. Remember that banks sometimes place a temporary hold on funds moving into your account from another source. Ask your closing agent how to make out the check. You can usually cover minor, last-minute adjustments in costs with your personal check.

Closing Documents

At closing you sign and receive the documents necessary to convey the new home to you and close the loan from the mortgage company (Figure 11.1). Those standard documents include the following items:

Deed. The deed conveys the home and lot to you, subject only to permitted exceptions such as a recorded easement.

Promissory Note. This note from you is payable to the lender in the principal amount of the loan, plus interest. Sign only one copy, unless you are willing to pay for your home more than once. You will sign and receive riders describing interest rate adjustments if you have that type of loan.

Mortgage or Deed of Trust. This document encumbers your home as security for repayment of the promissory note. Some states call this a mortgage, others a deed of trust. The result is the same: you must make your payments or risk losing your house.

Title Insurance Commitment. The title insurance company will mail you the actual policy in the weeks following your closing. When you receive this commitment, keep the

**Figure 11.1
Your Home
Involves
Numerous Closing
Documents**

document in a safe place with your other important papers. The document you see at closing simply promises to issue the policy. Title insurance is required in the amount of the mortgage to protect the lender if the title search missed anything. You are wise to request an owner's policy to protect your interest in the property. You can save a bit by ordering the owner's policy from the same company that issues the lender's policy. In some states, for an additional and modest fee, you can obtain mechanic's lien coverage also. This protection is not in the normal coverage, which doesn't make a lot of sense, because it is the most common problem that occurs. See Chapter 2 for details on liens.

Builder's Limited Warranty or Insurance-Backed Limited Warranty. Unless you move into your home early under a rental agreement with your builder, the limited warranty begins as of the date of closing. Although you should have received a copy of the warranty earlier, you sign and receive the official copy at closing. If your builder is providing an insurance policy to back the limited warranty, that insurance company will mail you additional documentation in the weeks following the closing.

Covenant-Protected Community. If your new home is in a covenant-protected community, your closing will include a review of home owners association covenants, conditions, and restrictions; the association by-laws; and articles of incorporation.

In addition to these standard items, the lender, title company, or builder may ask you to sign other documents. Although the clauses in them are not negotiable, you should know what they say. Subjects covered in separate documents might deal with radon, mold, your intention to use the new home as a primary residence, or confirmation that you have disclosed any secondary financing.

Closing Expenses

The closing agent itemizes the charges and credits for closing on a standardized form called a HUD-1 Settlement Statement (Figure 11.2). You are entitled by the Real Estate Settlement Procedures Act to review this completed form 24 hours before your closing appointment. You need only request a copy. The form appears daunting at first, but not every line applies to every closing. You can download a full-size copy from the U.S. Department of Housing and Urban Development's (HUD) web site. To find this form on line go to http://hudclips.org/. Under the word **forms,** click on Search or browse the **forms database.** Click on **HUD-11*.** The Settlement Statement is the first form in the list. You will need at least Acrobat 5.0 to access it. You probably will also want to download the instructions. The Settlement Statement also is available in Spanish.

The form lists standard items and has blank lines for additional entries specific to your purchase. The closing agent can answer questions about how amounts were calculated and describe each category. However, remember the closing agent has no authority to negotiate items. Amounts you paid during the processes of applying for the loan or building the home show up as credits to you on this summary. Common categories of charges you pay as closing costs include those described in the following paragraphs:.

Real Estate Commission (Line 700)

Usually expressed as a percentage in the contract, the exact dollar amount of applicable real estate commissions appears on the settlement statement. The names of the companies receiving the commissions, if any, appear as well. The use of a real estate agent is less common for a custom home than a production home.

Loan Items (Line 800)

Many of the charges you pay at closing relate to your new loan. Most were introduced in Chapter 2. The fees and charges vary, so you may encounter some not described here. These costs can appear to overlap, but if you understand each item, you won't worry that you are paying twice.

**Figure 11.2
Uniform
Settlement
Statement
(HUD-1)**

A. **Settlement Statement**

U.S. Department of Housing
and Urban Development

OMB Approval No. 2502-0265
(expires 9/30/2006)

B. Type of Loan

1. ☐ FHA 2. ☐ FmHA 3. ☐ Conv. Unins.
4. ☐ VA   5. ☐ Conv. Ins.

6. File Number:	7. Loan Number:	8. Mortgage Insurance Case Number:

C. **Note:** This form is furnished to give you a statement of actual settlement costs. Amounts paid to and by the settlement agent are shown. Items marked "(p.o.c.)" were paid outside the closing; they are shown here for informational purposes and are not included in the totals.

D. Name & Address of Borrower:	E. Name & Address of Seller:	F. Name & Address of Lender:

G. Property Location:	H. Settlement Agent:	
	Place of Settlement:	I. Settlement Date:

J. Summary of Borrower's Transaction		K. Summary of Seller's Transaction	
100. Gross Amount Due From Borrower		**400. Gross Amount Due To Seller**	
101. Contract sales price		401. Contract sales price	
102. Personal property		402. Personal property	
103. Settlement charges to borrower (line 1400)		403.	
104.		404.	
105.		405.	
Adjustments for items paid by seller in advance		Adjustments for items paid by seller in advance	
106. City/town taxes to		406. City/town taxes to	
107. County taxes to		407. County taxes to	
108. Assessments to		408. Assessments to	
109.		409.	
110.		410.	
111.		411.	
112.		412.	
120. Gross Amount Due From Borrower		**420. Gross Amount Due To Seller**	
200. Amounts Paid By Or In Behalf Of Borrower		**500. Reductions In Amount Due To Seller**	
201. Deposit or earnest money		501. Excess deposit (see instructions)	
202. Principal amount of new loan(s)		502. Settlement charges to seller (line 1400)	
203. Existing loan(s) taken subject to		503. Existing loan(s) taken subject to	
204.		504. Payoff of first mortgage loan	
205.		505. Payoff of second mortgage loan	
206.		506.	
207.		507.	
208.		508.	
209.		509.	
Adjustments for items unpaid by seller		Adjustments for items unpaid by seller	
210. City/town taxes to		510. City/town taxes to	
211. County taxes to		511. County taxes to	
212. Assessments to		512. Assessments to	
213.		513.	
214.		514.	
215.		515.	
216.		516.	
217.		517.	
218.		518.	
219.		519.	
220. Total Paid By/For Borrower		**520. Total Reduction Amount Due Seller**	
300. Cash At Settlement From/To Borrower		**600. Cash At Settlement To/From Seller**	
301. Gross Amount due from borrower (line 120)		601. Gross amount due to seller (line 420)	
302. Less amounts paid by/for borrower (line 220)	( )	602. Less reductions in amt. due seller (line 520)	( )
303. Cash ☐ From ☐ To Borrower		**603. Cash** ☐ To ☐ From Seller	

Section 5 of the Real Estate Settlement Procedures Act (RESPA) requires the following: • HUD must develop a Special Information Booklet to help persons borrowing money to finance the purchase of residential real estate to better understand the nature and costs of real estate settlement services; • Each lender must provide the booklet to all applicants from whom it receives or for whom it prepares a written application to borrow money to finance the purchase of residential real estate; • Lenders must prepare and distribute with the Booklet a Good Faith Estimate of the settlement costs that the borrower is likely to incur in connection with the settlement. These disclosures are manadatory.

Section 4(a) of RESPA mandates that HUD develop and prescribe this standard form to be used at the time of loan settlement to provide full disclosure of all charges imposed upon the borrower and seller. These are third party disclosures that are designed to provide the borrower with pertinent information during the settlement process in order to be a better shopper.

The Public Reporting Burden for this collection of information is estimated to average one hour per response, including the time for reviewing instructions, searching existing data sources, gathering and maintaining the data needed, and completing and reviewing the collection of information.

This agency may not collect this information, and you are not required to complete this form, unless it displays a currently valid OMB control number.

The information requested does not lend itself to confidentiality.

Previous editions are obsolete

Page 1 of 2

form HUD-1 (3/86)
ref Handbook 4305.2

**Figure 11.2
Uniform
Settlement
Statement
(HUD-1)
(*Continued*)**

L. Settlement Charges			
700. Total Sales/Broker's Commission based on price $ @ % =		Paid From Borrowers Funds at Settlement	Paid From Seller's Funds at Settlement
Division of Commission (line 700) as follows:			
701. $	to		
702. $	to		
703. Commission paid at Settlement			
704.			
800. Items Payable In Connection With Loan			
801. Loan Origination Fee	%		
802. Loan Discount	%		
803. Appraisal Fee	to		
804. Credit Report	to		
805. Lender's Inspection Fee			
806. Mortgage Insurance Application Fee to			
807. Assumption Fee			
808.			
809.			
810.			
811.			
900. Items Required By Lender To Be Paid In Advance			
901. Interest from to @$ /day			
902. Mortgage Insurance Premium for months to			
903. Hazard Insurance Premium for years to			
904. years to			
905.			
1000. Reserves Deposited With Lender			
1001. Hazard insurance months@$ per month			
1002. Mortgage insurance months@$ per month			
1003. City property taxes months@$ per month			
1004. County property taxes months@$ per month			
1005. Annual assessments months@$ per month			
1006. months@$ per month			
1007. months@$ per month			
1008. months@$ per month			
1100. Title Charges			
1101. Settlement or closing fee	to		
1102. Abstract or title search	to		
1103. Title examination	to		
1104. Title insurance binder	to		
1105. Document preparation	to		
1106. Notary fees	to		
1107. Attorney's fees	to		
(includes above items numbers:)			
1108. Title insurance	to		
(includes above items numbers:)			
1109. Lender's coverage	$		
1110. Owner's coverage	$		
1111.			
1112.			
1113.			
1200. Government Recording and Transfer Charges			
1201. Recording fees: Deed $; Mortgage $; Releases $			
1202. City/county tax/stamps: Deed $; Mortgage $			
1203. State tax/stamps: Deed $; Mortgage $			
1204.			
1205.			
1300. Additional Settlement Charges			
1301. Survey to			
1302. Pest inspection to			
1303.			
1304.			
1305.			
1400. Total Settlement Charges (enter on lines 103, Section J and 502, Section K)			

Note: To find this form on line got o http://hudclips.org/. Under the word forms, click on Search or browse the forms database. Click on HUD-1*. The Settlement Statement is the first form in the list. You will need at least Acrobat 5.0 to access it.

Origination Fee. This fee is a percentage of your loan amount, typically 1 percent. It pays your loan officer's compensation and the lender's administration costs. The amount of the origination fee was a negotiable item between you and your lender when you made your loan application. The Good Faith Estimate shows this percentage and the dollar amount. Unless your loan amount changed, the origination fee should match the figure listed on the Good Faith Estimate. The home buyer commonly pays this fee, but it is a negotiable item between the buyer and builder when the contract is signed.

Loan Discount or "Points." You pay this charge for interest up front, thereby reducing the interest rate on your loan. As explained in Chapter 2, one point equals 1 percent of the loan amount. One point reduces the interest rate about 1/8 of a percent, and the more points you pay, the lower your interest rate. Theoretically, a buyer could pay enough points to end up with a 0 percent loan. Anyone who could afford that would pay cash for the home and skip all this paperwork. Points are mortgage interest, and the amount is therefore usually deductible on your annual tax return.

Sometimes the builder pays the points as an incentive to buyers.

Appraisal Fee. You pay the cost of appraising the property. Government-assured Veterans Administration (VA) mortgages or Federal Housing Administration (FHA)-insured mortgages set the cost of the appraisal. The actual appraisal is a several-page document and may include photos showing your property and those to which the appraiser compared it.

Credit Report. You probably paid for your credit report when you applied for your loan. If so, that amount will appear as a credit. If you did not pay for it then, you will now. Lenders can require a second credit report if the original was issued more than a month before closing.

Lender's Inspection Fee. This amount covers the cost of a lender employee or outside agency inspecting your home during construction, at the point of each draw, and upon completion. Remember that these inspections confirm that work was completed. They do not guarantee quality or code compliance.

Mortgage Insurance Application Fee. If you made less than a 20-percent down payment and have a conventional loan, mortgage insurance is required for your loan. The administrative costs of processing your application appear as a charge to you.

Affidavits or Endorsements. More lenders are protecting themselves by obtaining written confirmation that the property and buyers meet all requirements. One example is a PUD (Planned Unit Development) endorsement that certifies you have followed all home owners association covenants. You pay a fee for the preparation and processing of such documents.

Lender Prepaids (Line 900)

The lender collects funds for several categories in advance, typically mortgage insurance (if applicable), hazard insurance, taxes, and interest. These prepaids can add up to a substantial amount.

Interest on the Loan. Except for the month in which your closing occurs, most loans are set up so that you pay interest in arrears, on the first of the next month in which the interest accrued. For example, if you close on June 27, you pay four days interest at the closing. On August 1, your first mortgage payment is due. This August 1 payment includes the interest that accrued during July.

Because the home buyer pays interest from the date of closing to the end of that month, 999 out of 1,000 closings take place during the last days of any given month. This payment practice reduces the amount of cash the buyers need for closing, although you end up paying it sooner or later. If possible, avoid the month-end rush and close earlier.

Mortgage Insurance Premium. Remember the mortgage insurance application fee you paid just a few lines ago? Because they approved you, you pay the first year's premium. This insurance picks up where you leave off if you default on your loan. You can understand how appealing this idea is to your lender. You do not need to die for it to take effect, so don't confuse it with credit life insurance, which does require your demise before it pays off the mortgage.

Hazard Insurance Premium. You will pay one year's worth of protection against loss by fire, wind, and other natural hazards. This coverage is usually part of the same home owner's policy that provides theft protection and liability protection in case your dog bites the mailman.

Reserves (Line 1000)

Often called escrow or impound accounts, these funds are held by the lender to pay future liabilities. For example, under the heading "Prepaids," you pay a year's premium on hazard insurance. The mortgage payment you send in each month will include 1/12 of the premium for renewing that insurance. That money is deposited into a reserve account by the lender. By the time the policy you pay for at closing comes up for renewal, you have deposited enough money to pay the renewal cost. The two to three months of reserve you pay at closing provides a margin of safety in the reserve account.

Mortgage insurance and taxes are processed the same way. A few loans allow you to pay these directly or offer you that choice. However, most people find paying them directly and forwarding proof of that payment to the lender is not worth the hassle.

Title Charges (Line 1100)

The work involved in transferring title to a property includes several steps and several people or companies. Naturally they expect payment for the work they perform on your behalf. The Uniform Settlement Statement (11.2) itemizes these charges.

Closing Fee. The people who administered this paperwork charge for their time and efforts.

Title Search. The title search confirms that the seller has the right to sell you the property you are buying and that no one else has any claim to it. This effort is the basis of the title insurance company's willingness to issue a title insurance policy.

Document Preparation or "Doc Prep." The pile of documents you are signing are the documents the closing agent assembled or prepared. When you see them, you will appreciate why they charge a separate fee for this.

Notary Fee. Usually a small charge, this fee certifies that the person signing your name to all this paperwork is really you. The settlement agent may require you to bring a driver's license or other photo identification.

Attorney's Fee. If one or more attorneys are involved in the closing, they will charge you for their time. If your attorney reviewed other documents throughout this transaction, you may already have taken care of this fee.

Lender's Title Insurance. This insurance protects the lender in case the title search missed anything. You pay for the title search and the one-time premium for the resulting insurance.

Owner's Title Insurance. This policy is similar to the lender's policy except that it protects you as the owner from loss if the title search missed any claims to the property. Give yourself the peace of mind this protection provides; the premium is a one-time charge.

Government Recording or Transfer Charges (Line 1200)

Counties collect fees when a property changes hands. Although this payment is negotiable between seller and buyer, the buyer usually pays the recording fees. The original contract describes the agreement you made.

Survey (Line 1301)

If the builder has not done so, the closing agent orders an improvement survey. The surveyor documents the property points and boundaries as well as showing where the home and other improvements are on the lot. Either the buyer or the seller pays the cost of the survey, as indicated in the contract.

Pest and Other Inspections (Line 1302)

A check for termites is the most common type of pest inspection. If your home is built in a region where termites are a concern, the builder will have included termite treatment in the building process. The lender will want this confirmed to allay fears the home might disappear in a feeding frenzy. Because this situation is actually possible in some locations, you are wise to keep up with this treatment.

Home Owners Association Fees

Your home owners association may impose some fees. The association sets these funds aside for maintaining and repairing common areas, operating recreational amenities, and so on. The builder sometimes pays a prorated portion as well.

Other Charges

You may see charges for messenger service, also called courier service, or Express Mail. And, of course, the cost of the house itself appears on this list. If you already owned your lot, the home closing process is simpler. Though not as simple as meeting the builder in a parking lot and exchanging a bag full of bills for house keys, you signed much of the paperwork described here when you closed on your lot purchase. Either way, after the closing, you may feel like you need to have yourself airlifted to the nearest hospital for emergency treatment for third-degree paper cuts. Hang on to your new house keys all the while. You now own your new home.

**Figure 11.3
Your Home Is
Finally Yours:
Celebrate!**

Moving In | 12

The activities of moving day differ from typical daily life. You may hear yourself asking questions such as, "Whose idea was this?" "Where'd we get all this stuff?" and "Did you bring the toilet paper like I asked you to?" In an unscientific survey of 3 billion people, not one listed moving as their favorite. On the other hand, moving is how you get from the old house to the new one, so let's get on with it. The checklists in Figures 12.1 through 12.3 can make moving a bit less chaotic.

Figure 12.1 Moving Preparation Checklist

☐ Compare proposals of professional movers.

   —Costs for services, insurance, distance, and weight charges
   —Availability and notice needed
   —Packing services
   —Packing materials

☐ Compare truck rentals for self-move.

   —Make truck reservation early.
   —Include a reservation for a dolly and moving pads.
   —Reconfirm one week before moving day.

☐ Involve your children in planning and preparing for the move.
☐ Create a file for storing documents about your home and manufacturer's literature.
☐ Retain receipts for tax purposes. Moving costs are sometimes deductible. Costs of improvements add to the "basis" cost of your home for the ultimate computation of your capital gains tax, where applicable.
☐ Send change-of-address cards to magazines and book clubs six weeks before your move.
☐ Give the forwarding order to your old post office one month prior to assure uninterrupted service.
☐ Arrange utility service in your name: water, sewer, gas, electric, telephone, cable television, trash collection, and security service.
☐ Register children in their new schools.
☐ Transfer medical and dental records, if necessary.
☐ Arrange for homeowner's insurance and obtain the certificate you need for closing.
☐ Order checks with your new address; update financial records.
☐ Update your driver's license and car and voter registrations.

Figure 12.2 Packing Materials Checklist

☐ Boxes of various sizes; cartons for mattresses

☐ Packing tape and heavy cord

☐ Packing paper, newspaper, Bubble Wrap®

☐ Labels to identify boxes (include a number, room/name)

☐ "Fragile" labels for special items

☐ Markers

☐ Master packing list (list each box by number with name/room and brief description of contents)

☐ Scissors

☐ Furniture pads, blankets, rugs

Before moving the first box or piece of furniture into your new home, inspect your home again for damage that may have occurred during work on last-minute items. Though not a common event, such damage can occur without your builder's knowledge. Notify the builder immediately and follow up in writing.

Next take precautions to protect vulnerable surfaces such as hardwood. Cover rails with moving pads or blankets. Remove doors where furniture is potentially a tight fit. Protect carpet with ribbed, plastic runners.

Professional movers should have insurance for any damage they cause. Friends and relatives will not. They are also unlikely to have the training and practiced skills of professional movers. If you are moving yourself, organize the schedule to avoid rushing and include rest breaks. People who are tired or in a hurry are more likely to hurt themselves or your belongings.

Whatever else is going on, at dinner time assemble the family for its first meal in the new home. Sit across the table from each other, smile, and say, "We made it" (Figure 12.4).

Figure 12.3 Moving Day Necessities Checklist

☐ Key to new home

☐ Address for and directions to the new home

☐ Children's toys and games

☐ Toilet paper

☐ Beverages and snacks

☐ Paper towels

☐ Soap and hand towels

☐ Trash bags (assorted sizes)

☐ First-aid kit

☐ Prescription medication

☐ Medical supplies for special needs

☐ Notepad and pen

☐ Scotch tape

☐ Shelf liners

☐ Small tools

   —Tape measure

   —Scissors

   —Screwdrivers

   —Hammer

☐ Ice maker hook-up kit

☐ Dryer vent flex hose

☐ New hoses for washing machine

☐ Picture hangers

☐ Plant hooks

☐ Scratch cover

☐ Cell phone

☐ Phone and electronic or paper phone book

**Figure 12.4
An Elegant
Doorway
Welcomes You
Home**

**Figure 12.5
Protect Hardwood
Floors and Carpet
During Move-In**

Your Home Care Plan   13
"What Do You Mean That's Not Covered by the Warranty?"

The smallest, simplest home contains thousands of parts, each performing according to intrinsic properties. Carpet, wood, concrete, and caulk behave in predictable ways. Not all these behaviors are desirable, but they are natural and many are inevitable. They result in normal maintenance tasks for home owners.

Your home requires care from day one. By planning maintenance from the beginning, you maximize your enjoyment of your home and the value of your investment. Think in terms of—

- routine care of surfaces with manufacturer-recommended products
- correct use and routine maintenance of systems
- replacement of consumable parts
- adjustment and lubrication of movable parts
- regular inspections

Many excellent books cover home maintenance in illustrated detail. Your builder may also provide specific information about your particular home's components. This chapter provides a practical approach to home maintenance and some examples of what is normal.

Read and Plan

Review the maintenance information your builder provides and all manufacturer's materials you receive. Though you have operated similar products in previous homes, small changes can prove significant. For example, without reading the manufacturer's literature about your new garbage disposal, you might not know that running cold water when you operate it cools the ball bearings and preserves the life of the motor. As you read the literature, start a seasonal schedule like the one in Figure 13.1.

Prepare for your home maintenance tasks by collecting the needed tools and materials. Maintenance is faster, easier, and more likely to get done on time if the necessary items are conveniently at hand. The consumable parts of your new home require regular replacement. Filters, light bulbs, batteries, weather stripping, and caulk are all examples. You are more likely to change the furnace filter regularly if you have a carton of them in the house.

Figure 13.1 Seasonal Maintenance Suggestions

Monthly (or per manufacturer's recommendations)

- [ ] Clean and test smoke alarms.
- [ ] Test and reset Ground Fault Circuit Interruption (GFCI) breakers.
- [ ] Change or clean heating, ventilation, air-conditioning (HVAC) filter(s).
- [ ] Drain sediment from water heater per manufacturer's instructions. (Local water quality determines needed frequency.)

Spring

- [ ] Check and operate air-conditioning system.
- [ ] Adjust registers and confirm that cold air returns are clear of furniture or draperies.
- [ ] Make certain the air-conditioner compressor is level and clear of debris.
- [ ] Turn the humidifier off.
- [ ] If your home has a private well, have the water tested.
- [ ] Start and adjust sprinkler system; test exterior faucets for broken pipes.
- [ ] Check overhead garage door, tighten bolts as needed, and lubricate springs with motor oil. Have other repairs done by professionals.
- [ ] Clean gutters and confirm that downspouts or splash blocks drain away from the house.
- [ ] Look for settling of backfill soils and fill in where needed.
- [ ] Check exterior caulking and touch up.
- [ ] Check exterior paint and stain surfaces (especially stained doors) and refinish as needed.
- [ ] Inspect grout around tile (floor or wall) and touch up.
- [ ] Wash windows and screens, clean weep holes, and lubricate tracks.
- [ ] Inspect for shrinkage damage such as minor drywall cracks and separations of wood trim. Repair as needed.
- [ ] Plan your first barbecue.

Summer

- [ ] Regularly check sprinkler head adjustments.
- [ ] Check interior caulking and touch up.
- [ ] Inspect grout around tile (floor or wall) and touch up.
- [ ] Pour a quart of water down the basement floor drain. As water in this drain evaporates, sewer fumes and odor can seep into the house.

Fall

- [ ] Operate the heating system.
- [ ] Adjust registers and confirm that cold air returns are clear of furniture or draperies.
- [ ] Clean the humidifier per manufacturer's instructions.
- [ ] Adjust or replace weatherstripping on exterior doors as needed.
- [ ] Check the fit of exterior doors at their thresholds. Many designs are adjustable; use a quarter to turn the large screws along the top edge.
- [ ] Drain your sprinkler system.
- [ ] Remove hoses from exterior faucets. Even "freeze-proof" faucets end up with a broken water line if the water in the hose freezes and expands into the pipe.
- [ ] Inspect chimney for nests.
- [ ] Review safe fireplace operation. Professional chimney cleaning [of chimney] is appropriate at yearly intervals for fireplaces and wood-burning stoves.
- [ ] Check overhead garage door, tighten bolts as needed, and lubricate springs with motor oil. Have other repairs done by professionals.
- [ ] Clean gutters, check downspouts, and confirm that splash blocks drain away from the house.
- [ ] Check foundation, concrete slabs, and yard for settling of backfill soils, fill in as needed to maintain drainage.
- [ ] Check exterior caulking and touch up.
- [ ] Wash windows and screens; lubricate tracks.

Winter

- [ ] Follow all instructions for safe operation of any fireplace or wood-burning stove.
- [ ] Brush snow off gutters and away from downspouts.
- [ ] Remove ice and snow from concrete surfaces as soon as possible.
- [ ] Avoid using de-icing agents with damaging salts.
- [ ] Conduct a radon test.
- [ ] Pour a quart of water down the basement floor drain. As water in this drain evaporates, sewer fumes and odor can seep into the house.
- [ ] On pleasant days, open windows to allow house to breathe.
- [ ] Decorate safely for the holidays; do not overload circuits or use worn extension cords.

Prompt Attention Keeps Minor Items Minor

Make prevention the hallmark of your home care plan. Providing minor attention immediately saves serious and time-consuming repairs later. A loose doorknob can scar the door surface if not tightened promptly. Negligence of routine maintenance can void applicable limited warranty coverage. Establishing a routine of regular, comprehensive inspection and attention prevents unnecessary expenses.

Do-It-Yourself or Professional?

Some home owners enjoy taking care of their homes. Others prefer to pay someone else to do the work. Either way is fine. Consider cost, your schedule, motivation, and skill level in deciding which items you will do and which you will hire others to do. Some work demands the services of a professional. One home owner saved the hassle of obtaining a permit and the cost of hiring a plumber to install a gas line to his fireplace. He and his wife died in the resulting explosion. Most of the time, home care is not a matter of life and death, but failure to respect the forces within a home can result in tragedy.

Your Home's Environment

When you think of environmental factors that affect your home, no doubt you think of weather first. Sun exposure, nearby bodies of water, traffic, or industry all affect your home's exterior surfaces. Elevation, orientation, and various pollutants are significant, too. In addition, the previous inhabitants of your lot, some with legs or wings and some with roots, may not depart when you arrive.

Critters

The county records office recognizes your ownership. Field mice, woodpeckers, ants, bees, and other indigenous life may not. When one company built homes across an established deer trail, the deer continued to follow their traditional path—right through yards and gardens, occasionally pausing for a light snack. Whether entertaining or threatening, one thing these creatures have in common is that they are yours to contend with.

Before taking any action against native animal life, check applicable laws; some of these creatures enjoy legal protection.

A notable exception are termites. In some areas, builders treat the house foundation for termites and provide a certificate confirming that treatment. In that case your responsibility is to renew this treatment when appropriate. For help with other critters that make holes (squirrels or woodpeckers) or threaten safety (hornets or wasps) or convenience (skunk), look to your county cooperative extension service, animal control, or the public library.

Mildew

In some climates, keeping mildew under control is an ongoing battle. Mildew, a fungus that spreads through the air in microscopic spores, loves moisture and feeds on surfaces or dirt. On siding, it looks like a layer of dirt. Check with your builder, local paint contractor, or siding company for a recipe that removes mildew. Always wear your best protective eyewear and rubber gloves for this task. The chemicals that remove mildew are unfriendly to humans as well.

Mold

Mold exists naturally in our environment and can grow on many surfaces within a home if conditions are right. Mold needs an organic food source (such as wood), moisture, air, and moderate temperatures. The only one of these your builder or you can control within your home is moisture. Should a leak occur, report it immediately for warranty attention, or if the cause is unrelated to warranty (such as a hole in the roof from those terrific holiday decorations or that caulking around the tub that needs to be maintained), take immediate action yourself to prevent the growth of mold. If you regularly inspect your home and take prompt action if any moisture concerns develop, you are unlikely to experience any difficulty with mold.

Caulking and Tile Grout. Maintain all caulking around such areas as windows, doors, sinks, and tubs. Inspect and maintain grout as a seal to keep moisture from reaching the wall behind the tile.

Cleaning. Vacuum and dust regularly because mold grows well on dust and dirt. Clean or replace filters frequently (at minimum according to the manufacturer's recommendations). Keep weep holes for brick and windows clear. Promptly clean up spills, condensation, and other sources of moisture. Do not let water pool or stand in your home. Thoroughly dry any wet surfaces or material. Many bath tile cleaning products contain chemicals that remove and help protect against mold growth.

If mold develops, thoroughly clean the affected area, but first, test to see if the affected material or surface will be harmed by the cleaning solution you chose. (Wear rubber gloves and safety glasses.) Promptly replace any materials that you cannot thoroughly dry, such as drywall or insulation. Discard porous materials, such as fabric, upholstery, or carpet. For severe mold growth, call on the services of a qualified professional cleaner.

Condensation. If you notice condensation, wipe it up and reduce the humidity level in your home. For example, if your home includes a humidifier, turn it down or off. Also operate and clean it according to the manufacturer's instructions. Use the hood fan in the kitchen when cooking and the bathroom fan when bathing or showering.

Inspections. Check your home regularly for signs of water intrusion such as a musty odor, staining, or actual standing moisture. Check inside cabinets, under all sinks, behind toilets, and in seldom-used closets. If applicable, confirm that your sump pump functions correctly. Check weather stripping, caulking, grout, weep holes, and so on. Check the refrigerator pan, air-conditioning condensate line, coils, and condenser pan for signs of mold growth. Keep the clothes dryer exhaust tube clear and functioning efficiently. Make sure nothing covers or interferes with the fresh air supply for the furnace.

Landscaping and Drainage. Maintain positive drainage around your home. Avoid changes to the grade or exterior additions that interfere with drainage away from the home. Avoid edgings or borders that dam water near the home. Regularly inspect any sprinkler system for correct function. Adjust sprinkler heads to water the lawn not the house and correct any leaks immediately. Keep splashblocks or downspout extensions in place to channel roof water away from your home. Clean gutters as needed to prevent overflow. (Splashblocks catch and sometimes slow rainwater running out of downspouts.)

Leaks. Be familiar with the shut off valves for all water supply lines in your home. In the event of a leak, immediately—

- Shut off the water at the appropriate valve to minimize the amount of water that is released.
- Clean up the water.
- Report any leak to your builder including roof, window, or plumbing leaks. Failure to report leaks promptly increases your risk and responsibility for repairs.

Purchases or Stored Items. Carefully inspect items you bring into your home such as boxes that have been in storage or new house plants for any sign of mold, including musty odors.

Health Effects. For some susceptible persons, exposure to mold has been shown to cause allergic reactions. However, the level of any reactive exposure varies greatly, depending on the individual. While some have suggested a link between mold exposure and serious disease, this assertion has not been supported by scientific and medical research. Both the Centers for Disease Control and the National Academy of Sciences state that no causal link exists between the presence of mold and serious health conditions. For more information on the health effects associated with mold, visit these two websites—

- Centers for Disease Control, at www.cdc.gov/nceh/airpollution/mold/pib.pdf (When you get to the website click on *A-Z Index,* the letter *M,* and *Mold.* That page provides links to reports, press releases, projects, and even congressional testimony.)
- National Academy of Sciences (NAS), www.nationalacademies.org/topnews (To get to a news brief, click on edit, find, and type in the word *mold.* The news brief provides links to the full report and a press release.)

Neighbors

Whether adjacent lots were occupied when your home was built or your neighbors arrived after you did, neighborhood friendships are important. Community watch and recycling programs are increasingly common. Recreational amenities and organized social programs are a benefit in covenant-protected communities with active associations.

In getting settled, however, neighbors sometimes create problems for one another by installing fences, patios, pools, decks, or gardens. In one case, a man planted a row of trees along his drive and drastically altered the drainage between his and a neighbor's home. The result was a wet basement—for the neighbor. Resolving such concerns is a task for the individuals involved and possibly the home owners association.

Your Lot

The soil on your lot influences more than just the foundation design. Topography (surface shape), as well as the soil's ability to absorb water and support plant life, become significant parts of your planning. Natural features inspire your landscape design, and an unadorned site challenges your imagination.

Your ideal yard may take many years to perfect (Figure 13.2). Planning your landscaping in stages allows you to spread the cost over several seasons. As soon as possible, cover

Photo by James F. Wilson, Dallas, Texas.

the ground to prevent erosion. If your builder provided landscaping, you have escaped only the first round of work. Yards that flourish result from consistent attention.

Maintaining drainage away from your home is critical to protect your foundation and keep the basement dry. Failing to maintain adequate drainage can cause serious damage and void your structural warranty. Remember how the excavation for your home was larger than the foundation to allow room to work? As this backfill area settles, restore the soil to its original level with fill dirt. Figure 13.3 lists other yard care hints that apply to most regions.

Settling

All building materials expand and contract with changes in temperature and humidity. Houses adjust constantly to the differences in temperature between the interior and exterior. Some climates have extreme differences, from morning to night and season to season. When we think of a new home, lumber, drywall, and paint come to mind. Few of us think of water. Yet water is abundant in concrete, drywall texture, and paint. Precipitation during construction can contribute more moisture.

Dissimilar materials—for example, wood trim installed over drywall or bricks abutting siding—expand and contract at different rates in response to these fluctuations. The result is a slight separation between the two materials. This separation is evident in drywall cracks, separations where moldings meet walls, or at mitered corners of door casings. Doors may require adjustments because of these changes. This situation can alarm new home owners, but it's normal behavior for these materials. These effects are most noticeable during the first year and can continue beyond that. Caulk or paint is often all you need to correct the evidence of this natural process.

Some authorities estimate new homes contain as much as 50 gallons of water. By comparison, an average family of four generates 3 to 6 gallons of water per day through the activities of daily living.

Figure 13.3 Landscaping Hints

- Create a long-term plan that you can implement in stages.
- Consider a Xeriscape™ approach (low water-consuming, locally acclimated plants).*
- Cover soil as soon as possible to prevent erosion.
- Maintain proper slope away from your home for good drainage.
- Avoid altering drainage swales when preparing the soil for seed or sod, digging holes for shrubs, or raking the soil.
- Provide good soil mixes with sufficient organic material.
- Plant vegetation suited to your local climate.
- Consider ultimate size, shape, and growth of the species you plant.
- Space trees to allow for efficient mowing and growth. Consider shading and windbreak benefits when planting trees.
- Group plants with similar water, sun, and space requirements.
- Make provisions for efficient irrigation.
- Do not allow edgings around decorative rock or bark beds to dam water against the home.
- Use 3 inches of mulch to hold soil moisture and prevent weeds.
- Check sprinkler performance weekly; direct heads away from the home.
- Apply appropriate fertilizer and weed and pest controls for optimum growth. Use organic compounds for additional protection of the environment.

* Xeriscape is a registered trademark of Denver Water, Denver, CO, and is used here with permission. The seven principles of Xeriscape include planning and design, limiting turf, improving soil, zoning plants, mulching, irrigating efficiently, and doing appropriate maintenance, see www.xeriscape.org.

Caulk

Over time caulk dries, shrinks, and cracks. Once this happens its effectiveness diminishes and it no longer seals out moisture and air. This change is most noticeable during the first year or two because of natural expansion and contraction of dissimilar materials combined with the settling activities of a new home. Some builders provide a one-time touch-up as part of their customer service program. You need to touch up caulking inside and out as needed as part of your ongoing maintenance. Hardware and home stores carry caulking compounds and dispenser guns. Read manufacturer's labels carefully to select caulk appropriate to the task:

- Silicone or polyurethane caulks work best in areas that get wet—for example, where bathtub meets tile. Read the label carefully. You cannot paint over all types of caulk.
- Latex caulk is appropriate for areas that require painting, such as where stairs meet wall.
- Colored caulk is available where larger selections are provided.

Concrete

Concrete cracks. This annoying trait results from shrinkage as the concrete cures (approximately half an inch in a 10-foot width), from temperature changes, soil movement, or heavy vehicles. You can prevent some cracks and minimize others, but you can't prevent them all. Control joints (grooves in the surface) create a weak spot, and we all hope any cracks occur in those joints. The concrete does not always cooperate with this plan. Some hints when caring for concrete include the following:

- Maintain good drainage away from concrete slabs.
- Fill low spots or settled areas near concrete slabs.
- Seal cracks with a flexible concrete caulking to prevent moisture from getting under the slab.
- Remove ice and snow as soon as possible.
- Protect concrete from de-icing agents (such as road salt), pet urine, fertilizers, and radiator overflow. These substances cause the surface to chip.
- Keep heavy vehicles such as moving vans or delivery trucks off your driveway.

Drywall

Once installed, taped, textured, and painted, the drywall in your home pretty much just hangs there. However, other forces can act upon it to produce a variety of maintenance tasks. Slight cracking, *nail pops,* or seams may become visible in walls and ceilings. Shrinkage of the wood and normal deflection of rafters can cause these annoyances. A nail pop occurs when the wood the nail is in shrinks and squeezes the nail part of the way out. Cracking along a *corner bead* is also common. A corner bead is a metal edge the installer uses to create neat corners. As the house settles, corner beads can pop out of position. Many builders provide repairs to these items one time during the warranty year. After that, they become your maintenance task.

Systems

Expect the mechanical systems in your new home to perform differently from those in previous homes. Each home is unique in the way it interacts with wind currents, passive solar effects, its orientation to its neighbors, and surrounding plant life. Each installation also is different, even if the same trade contractor does the work. Learn how to operate your new systems to maximize their efficiency and your family's comfort. Know where the main shutoffs are for water, electricity, and gas.

Heating System

The furnace blower cycles on and off more frequently and for shorter periods during severe cold spells. Avoid overheating your new home; this practice increases shrinkage in framing lumber and may materially damage the house. At first, use as little heat as possible and increase it gradually. Furnaces installed in basements typically have combustion air vents run to them. Never cover these or block the cold air in any way. The furnace and other utilities or appliances need an air supply to operate safely. Blocking the combustion air vent can cause the furnace to draw air down the vent pipe, pulling poisonous gases back into your home.

Air-Conditioning

Home air-conditioning continually recycles and cools the air until it reaches the desired temperature. Unlike a light bulb that reacts instantly when you turn on a switch, the air-conditioning unit begins the process only when you lower the thermostat setting. If you come home at 5:30 p.m. when the temperature is 95 degrees and set your thermostat to 72 degrees, the air-conditioner begins the cooling process. But during the day the sun has been heating the air in the house, the walls, the carpet, and the furniture. As the system starts cooling the air, the walls, carpet, and furniture release heat and nullify the effect. Allow the unit to maintain a moderate temperature through the day; you can always lower the setting slightly when you arrive home.

Ventilation

Homes today are built more tightly than ever. This practice saves energy dollars, but it creates a potential concern. Condensation, cooking odors, indoor pollutants, radon, and carbon monoxide all may accumulate. We have mechanical and passive methods available for ventilating homes and the task is important to health and safety.

Gases that are by-products of combustion in fireplaces, gas furnaces, water heaters, and clothes dryers should go out through a chimney or vent pipe. As these warm gases rise in the chimney, a vacuum forms in the home. Since few openings exist for air to enter, this vacuum can reverse the flow of the gases, pulling them into the home. Carbon monoxide, an odorless and colorless component of these gases, causes headaches, nausea, fatigue, fainting, brain damage, and even death. You can purchase an alarm designed to detect carbon monoxide for $30 to $60 at hardware stores. Follow instructions carefully for installation.

Radon, another invisible and odorless gas, forms as a by-product of decaying uranium. Depending on local geology and weather, radon can enter any house. Winter is the best time to test for its presence, and reputable test kits are available at a nominal cost. Follow directions carefully and average the results of two or more tests several weeks apart. If results show that significant amounts of radon are present, take corrective steps, including installing a vent pipe and fans.

Unoccupied areas need ventilation also. Attic ventilation occurs through vents in the soffit (the underside of the overhangs) or on gable ends. Driving rain or snow sometimes enter the attic through gable vents. Do not cover them to prevent this. Instead, cover the insulation in front of the vent. Precipitation that blows in safely evaporates and ventilation can still occur. Building codes require these vents as well as vents for crawl spaces to minimize accumulation of moisture.

Besides features built into your home, your daily habits can help keep your home well-ventilated:

- Do not cover or interfere in any way with the fresh air supply to your furnace.
- Develop the habit of running the hood fan when you are cooking.
- Ditto the bath fans when bathrooms are in use.
- Air your house by opening windows for a time when weather permits.

Also be aware that recent feedback from home owners (in both old and new houses) regarding black sooty stains that develop on surfaces in homes (on carpet, walls, ceilings, appliances, mirrors, and around area rugs—to list a few examples) have caused much investigation and research.

The conclusion of the research and laboratory tests has been that the majority of this staining or "ghosting" results from pollution of the air in the home caused by burning

Incomplete combustion of hydrocarbons in scented candles can causes sooty stains or "ghosting" on home surfaces.

scented candles. Incomplete combustion of hydrocarbons as these candles burn contributes a considerable amount of soot to the air. This soot then settles on surfaces of the home. The sooty deposits are extremely difficult to remove; on some surfaces (light-colored carpet, for instance), they are impossible to remove completely.

The popularity of scented candles has increased many fold in recent years. If this activity is part of your lifestyle, use caution and consider the potential damage to your home. When this condition results from home owners burning candles or other lifestyle choices, the resulting damage is excluded from the builder's warranty coverage.

Plumbing

If the plumbing in the home you are leaving gurgles and swishes, you probably seldom notice. Your new home will produce different noises that may sound strange at first. The time required for hot water to reach each sink in the home may also vary from what you are accustomed to. Your new plumbing system contains many water-saving devices. New shower heads contain flow restrictors you cannot remove. Government regulations for water conservation now limit toilet manufacturers to designs that use 1.6 gallons of water for each flush. Figure 13.4 lists hints for those concerned with freezing pipes.

Electrical

Breakers have three positions: on, off, and tripped. When a breaker trips, move it first to the off position and then return it to the on position. Switching directly from tripped to on does not restore power. Figure 13.5 suggests steps to follow if an outlet fails to provide power.

Ground Fault Circuit Interrupters (GFCI). These indoor circuit breakers sense fluctuations in power and trip to prevent electrocution. Building codes require GFCI protec-

---

Figure 13.4 Hints for Freezing Pipes

If temperatures in your area dip unusually low, freezing pipes, especially those in exterior walls, may become a concern. Should your pipes freeze, the hints that follow may help:

- Do not lower heat below 60 degrees.
- During extremely cold periods, or if you will be away, leave cabinet doors open under sinks to allow warm air to circulate.
- If power is interrupted, turn faucets on and allow water to drip slowly to prevent freezing.
- If you discover your pipes have frozen, use a hair dryer to thaw them. Do not use a torch or hot water.
- If you decide to finish the basement, take care to ensure that plumbing lines are not isolated from the heating source without benefit of insulation.
- Keep garage doors closed to protect plumbing lines that run through this area.

Figure 13.5 Electrical Outlets

If an outlet is not working, check—

- to see if it is one controlled by a wall switch (usually found in bedrooms)
- the Ground Fault Circuit Interrupter (GFCI) controls for that outlet
- the breaker in the main breaker panel

If a circuit trips repeatedly, unplug all items connected to it and reset the breaker. If it trips when nothing is plugged in, leave it off and contact an electrician. If the circuit remains on, one of the items you unplugged is defective and requires repair or replacement.

tion for outlets in bathrooms, the kitchen, outside, and in the garage. One GFCI breaker can control several outlets. Once a month press each GFCI test button. You find this on one of the outlets for each GFCI circuit. The circuit should go off. To restore service, press the reset button. If a GFCI breaker trips during normal use you may have a faulty appliance. Do not plug a refrigerator or food freezer into a GFCI-controlled outlet. If a defective lamp or small appliance triggers the GFCI to shut off, the contents of the refrigerator or the freezer could spoil. None of your warranties cover this possibility.

Smoke Detectors. Smoke detectors are one of the most important components of your electrical system. They are wired directly into your home's electrical system, and many include a battery for back up. A chirping sound indicates the battery is weak and should be replaced. Regular cleaning is imperative to their proper functioning. Test them regularly by pushing the test button on each unit. The alarm should sound. If it does not, call for service immediately.

Cosmetic Surfaces

Habits that prevent damage such as scratches, chips, cuts, burns, stains, gouges, and scrapes preserve the appearance and life of the cosmetic surfaces of your home. To counter the accumulated effects of time and normal living activities, regular cleaning and attention are also essential. But from time to time you must take more aggressive actions.

Paint

Years ago paint contained chemicals such as lead that made it dangerous for people, especially young people. Because of increased awareness of these dangers and corresponding regulations, manufacturers have removed these ingredients from paint formulas. What is

Touching up painted surfaces usually produces more satisfactory results than scrubbing.

left is safer but not as washable. Home owners who wash their painted walls see the water-soluble paint and sometimes drywall texture (which is also water soluble) come off on the sponge and conclude their builder has cut corners. In fact, the builder and paint manufacturer merely complied with current regulations. Most of today's flat paints will tolerate only gentle cleaning.

Carpet

Expect to see some or all of the following normal traits in your new carpet: seams, *roll crush*, filtration, and bags of lint in your vacuum. Seams are visible because of the heat tape under the edges of the carpet. The heat tape includes a layer of glue. During installation, the carpet installer uses an iron-like device to melt the glue, binding the two edges together. The heat tape under the carpet pushes the carpet up a bit. When light hits it, the seam is visible. Over time, traffic and vacuuming make the seam less noticeable.

Roll crush occurs when carpet is rolled and stored. The bottom of the roll gets squished and takes longer to fluff up after unrolling. Filtration occurs if you keep doors closed while operating the HVAC system. As air is drawn under the doors, the carpet filters some of the pollution out of the air and a dingy stripe forms at the threshold. The lint your vacuum collects proves your carpet is new. Depending on how often you vacuum, this harmless effect could last for months.

Balance manufacturer claims that carpet is soil-resistant with a healthy respect for the influence children and pets wield. Nothing can show up science and chemistry quite like an active 4-year-old. Traffic paths develop over time. One carpet expert shocked me during a warranty visit by stating that the oil from the bottom of bare feet contributes to traffic paths. Levitation seems to be the only means to completely protect our carpets.

Resilient Flooring

Avoid excessive water, which will penetrate seams and cause the edges of your flooring to lift and curl. Use caution when moving appliances across resilient floor covering. Putting a piece of carpet with the nap down under the legs of heavy items helps protect the flooring. I wish I had remembered this when we moved our refrigerator into our first new home. The two gouges, 2 inches by 6 inches, looked like meteor craters to me. The resulting patch, which I had to pay for, was not readily noticeable and held up without problems the entire eight years we owned the home. This experience is better avoided, however, so remember that carpet. Coasters for furniture legs help prevent damage from day-to-day movements.

Hardwood Floor

Imagine how your coffee table would look if you walked on it. If your wood floor has a polyurethane finish, in six months to a year have a qualified contractor apply another coat. Check with your hardwood company for specific care guidelines for your particular floor. Some additional tips follow:

- Wood floors respond noticeably to changes in the humidity level in a home, especially during the winter. A humidifier helps but does not completely eliminate this reaction.
- When new, small splinters of wood may appear.
- Moving furniture or dropping heavy or sharp object causes dimples or scratches.
- Expect some shrinkage or warping around heat vents or any heat-producing appliances.
- Excessive water damages any floor. Wood flooring can warp if it becomes wet repeatedly or is thoroughly soaked even one time.
- Moisture can cause a white, filmy appearance.

- When damp-mopping, squeeze all excess water from the mop.
- A dulling of the finish in heavy traffic areas is likely.
- Heels that have lost their protective cap will mar the floor.

Movable Parts

A home contains many moving parts. Windows and doors open and close, kitchen drawers slide, knobs turn, locks lock, and registers adjust. Through use, some of these get out of adjustment or require cleaning and lubrication. Refer to manufacturer suggestions to use for specific products. Generally, silicone or graphite products make good lubricants; oil-based products become sticky and attract dirt.

Windows

In heavy rains, water collects in the bottom channel of window frames. Weep holes, small slits in the frame, allow it to escape. Keep these clean. Most sliding windows (both vertical and horizontal) are designed for a 10-pound pull. A silicone lubricant helps if sticking becomes a problem. Patio door tracks operate smoothly when clean. Wax is a good lubricant.

Overhead Garage Door

The garage door is a large, moving object and the vibrations from operating it can loosen the bolts. Periodic maintenance combined with adherence to manufacturer's instructions ensures safe and reliable operation. The door springs are under potentially dangerous tension so have a qualified specialist make any needed adjustments. Have a professional garage door technician inspect the door if it receives any significant impact. Listed below are some other cautions to keep in mind:

- Keep hands and fingers away from all parts of the door except the handle.
- Do not allow children to play with, or around, the door.
- Every six months, apply a 30-weight automobile oil or a similar lubricant to moving parts: track, rollers, hinges, pulleys, and springs. Make sure hardware is tight and operating as intended without binding or scraping.

Warranty

From the first day of ownership, your lifestyle affects your home. You'll want your family's daily activities to protect and preserve it. You do not place a hot iron on a laminated countertop or permit your 3-year-old to crayon on the walls—at least not with your knowledge. At routine intervals, you need to take specific actions to keep your home looking and performing its best. These range from installing a clean furnace filter to repainting the exterior.

During the time covered by the various warranties, if your daily care and routine maintenance do not keep the home in working order, one of several warranties probably applies. You therefore should view understanding and using your warranty coverage as an important component of your home care plan.

Warranty Service

"I Just Have a Short List"

14

Builders, trade contractors, and manufacturers strive to produce homes that are defect-free and easy to maintain. They also realize that installation errors occur and materials do not always perform as expected. Consequently, when you purchase a new home, a warranty bouquet comes with it. This bouquet, which is sometimes confusing, consists of warranties of various durations and from several sources: implied warranties provided by state laws, express (oral or written) warranty provided by the builder, trade contractor and manufacturer warranties, and possibly third-party insurance coverage to back the builder warranty.

Whatever the particular combination of warranties that apply to your home, the components should meet accepted standards during the warranty period. If something does not, one or more warranties apply. You maximize the protection from these warranties if you—

- read and retain all warranty documents
- provide recommended maintenance for all parts of your property
- follow claim procedures carefully
- maintain an accurate history of all work done on your home

Implied Warranty

Virtually all states recognize implied warranties to some extent. Implied warranties are based on state statutes and on case law, or precedent. The theory behind an implied warranty obligation is that a buyer is entitled to believe that no builder would knowingly sell a defective product. Under implied warranties builders are assumed to make certain commitments to their home buyers, such as the home being "fit for the intended use" or that it will be "habitable." These assumptions apply whether or not the builder provides an express (oral or written) warranty. Specific coverages and requirements vary from state to state and can change as cases move through the legal system.

The terms of many of the limited warranties builders provide include an agreement to waive these implied warranties. However, some states may not permit this waiver. If a legal confrontation occurs and the builder's warranty is judged equitable, the court probably will enforce it. However, if the court deems that the builder's warranty is unfair, the judge may set aside its terms and rely on state laws to resolve the dispute.

New Home Limited Warranty

One of the most important warranties you receive is the new home limited warranty your builder provides. Over 90 percent of builders provide a written warranty. Whether in writing or oral, these express warranties are considered stated, as opposed to the implied warranty provided by state laws.

The new home limited warranty you get from your builder warranties is either builder-backed or insurance-backed. If builder-backed, it is termed self-insured, meaning that the builder's resources back the limited warranty. If the builder's warranty commitment is insured by a separate insurance company, that company also backs the limited warranty. (See "Insured Warranty Policies" for more details.)

Whether builder-backed or insurance-backed, the new home warranty describes the terms and conditions of the coverage your builder provides. To prevent misunderstandings, this warranty should be in writing. If your builder does not provide a specimen copy at the time you sign your contract, request one. Read it carefully. Ask for an explanation of any details you do not understand. Three types of coverage are common in new home limited warranties: materials and workmanship, systems, and structural.

Materials and Workmanship Coverage

The warranty for materials and workmanship is the most used of those that come with your home. Although a few two-year programs exist, this coverage usually extends for one year. Many builders provide written standards for this part of the limited warranty. These standards list common warranty items, set criteria for judging them, and describe the correction the builder provides if they occur. You can review two examples in Figure 14.1.

As the home owner, you are responsible for normal maintenance. But if part of the home behaves in a way that exceeds the warranty tolerance or if an installer erred in assembling materials, the materials and workmanship warranty applies. For instance, carpet requires regular vacuuming to look its best. This task is maintenance and therefore your job. If clumps of the yarn pull out, revealing the carpet backing, the material may be defective and the manufacturer may be obligated to your builder to replace it. If a seam comes apart, the workmanship may be faulty. The installation company may be responsible for correcting this problem through its contract with your builder.

Repairs of damages caused by living in the home are your responsibility just as fixing a dented fender is if you drive your car into a tree. If you drop the roaster into the kitchen sink on Thanksgiving Day, the builder does not repair the chip. However, if the sprayer dribbles when the faucet is running, the builder arranges for the repair.

Systems Coverage

Systems warranty coverage for two years is less prevalent, although most insured warranties cover this time period. The systems warranty covers the in-the-wall parts of the electrical, plumbing, and heating and air-conditioning systems. Systems coverage may not include fixtures. For instance, wires, pipes, and ducts are covered; the nook light, the bathroom sink, and registers may fall under only the materials and workmanship warranty. If systems coverage is not part of your builder's limited warranty, your materials and workmanship

Figure 14.1 Sample Builder Limited Warranty Guidelines

Air-Conditioning

When the home includes air-conditioning, the system should maintain a temperature of 78 degrees or a differential of 15 degrees from the outside temperature, measured in the center of each room at a height of five (5) feet above the floor. Lower temperature settings are often possible but neither the manufacturer nor the [Builder] promise performance at that level.

Nonemergency

Lack of air-conditioning service is not an emergency. The heating and air-conditioning contractor responds to reports of problems in the order received.

Coolant

The outside temperature must reach 70 degrees or higher for the contractor to add coolant to the system.

Compressor

The air-conditioning compressor must remain level. If it settles during the first year, the [Builder] will correct this. After the first year, the Home Owner must maintain it.

Cabinets

Cabinets should operate properly under normal use. Doors, drawer fronts, and handles should stay level and even.

Warping

The [Builder] will correct warped doors or drawer fronts if warpage exceeds 1/8" within 24" separations.

The [Builder] will correct gaps between cabinets and ceiling or cabinets and walls by caulking or other means if they exceed 1/8" (locations behind appliances excepted).

Wood Grain

Readily noticeable variations in wood grain and color are expected in all style selections. The [Builder] does not provide replacements to such variations.

Surface Damage

The [Builder] will correct chips, scratches, and other surface flaws noted on the orientation list.

warranty covers the systems for the time period it remains in effect (usually one year). Claims under systems warranties are less common than material and workmanship claims.

Structural Coverage

In this context, structural means the parts of the house that hold up its weight. These parts include such items as the foundation, floor joists, beams, rafters, and trusses. This distinction is an important one. Many home owners misunderstand structural warranty coverage. This coverage protects against potentially dangerous, catastrophic structural damage. For instance, a structural warranty does not cover a crack in a walkway that does not hold up any weight. Structural coverage is especially important in areas of the country where unstable soil conditions exist. The period of coverage varies from 1 to 10 years depending on regional construction conditions and the builder.

Obligations and Limitations

A new home warranty should clearly state the obligations of the builder and the home owner, as well as list exclusions. The builder is typically obligated to repair, replace, or pay the home owner the reasonable cost of repairing or replacing the defective item. Often the builder's total liability under this warranty is limited to the purchase price of the home.

Understanding what is not provided by your new home warranty is as important as knowing what is provided.

Note that the choice among repair, replacement, or payment is the builder's. Steps taken by the builder to correct defects do not extend the term of this warranty. Warranty repairs provided by the builder are at no charge to the home owner and should be performed within a reasonable length of time.

A typical home owner obligation entry requires that the home owner provide normal maintenance and proper care of the home, notify the builder in writing of any warranty item, and provide the builder with access to home during normal business hours to inspect the item reported and, if necessary, to take corrective action (Figure 14.2).

Categories of items not covered by a limited warranty are called exclusions. One item typically excluded is consequential or incidental damages. If a roof leak occurs, the builder repairs the roof leak and damage to the ceiling or walls. However, damage to your television is consequential and is not covered by the builder's warranty. Some states do not allow the exclusion of consequential damages. In addition to the exclusion of consequential damages, a new home warranty might list other excluded categories:

- defects in any item that was not part of the original home
- any defect caused by lack of proper maintenance
- normal wear and tear
- acts of God, including such events as windstorms, lightning, floods, and earthquakes
- any damage caused by changes in the grading or drainage patterns or by excessive watering
- failure of the home owner to take action to minimize damage and give notice of the defect
- insect or animal damage

**Figure 14.2
Home Owners
Must Maintain
Their Homes
Including Such
Features as This
Patio Kitchen and
Fireplace**

Photo by James F. Wilson, Dallas, Texas.

Trade Contractors' Warranties

Under the terms of their contracts with the builder, trade contractors typically warranty their workmanship and any materials they provide for one year. Builders monitor the quality of work and materials that trade contractors provide. Their performance affects the builder's future decisions about which trade contractors to use. In most cases, because of the builder's responsibility to you, if a trade contractor goes out of business, the builder still provides repairs for covered warranty items. For this reason and others, builders prefer to work with trade contractors they know and trust.

Manufacturer's Warranties

Your builder passes through or assigns consumer product warranties to you. Keep all manufacturer warranties and literature. Coverage provided by these warranties on some parts of the house may exceed the protection provided by the builder's limited warranty on materials and workmanship. For example, furnace warranties typically cover the heat exchanger for 10 years (parts only, you pay labor). Manufacturers may offer extended service agreements on some products. Expect to find your mailbox full of such offers for months after you move in.

A 1975 federal law, the Magnuson-Moss Act, sets disclosure requirements for those who sell consumer products. For the purposes of this law, consumer products include such items as dishwashers, furnaces, and air-conditioners. The law requires that consumers have access to the manufacturer warranties on these products before they make a purchasing decision. Some production builders assemble a notebook of these warranties in the sales office. Others post a copy beside the product in the model home. Because custom buyers can purchase their consumer products anywhere, the responsibility for making manufacturer warranties available shifts to the store in which the buyers view the products.

Insured Warranty Policies

Insured warranty coverage offers additional protection. If your builder belongs to an insurance-backed warranty program, the premiums add to the cost of your home just as the addition of any other feature does. The insurance company reviews the builder's credentials before accepting homes into the insurance program. At the start of construction, the builder registers your home, which the insurer may inspect during construction. After closing and receipt of the final premium, the insurance company issues the policy and mails a copy to the home owner. Most of these policies allow that protection to transfer to subsequent owners.

During the first and second year of the material and workmanship and systems coverage, the insurance assures that the builder complies with the insurer's written standards on covered items. The builder must provide repairs for any items that do not meet these standards. If the builder cannot or will not provide covered repairs, the home owner has recourse through the insurance carrier. Note that this insurance protects you according to the standards listed in the insurance policy, not your personal standards.

Structural insured warranty coverage provides protection for the home owner and the builder. Under some policies, structural coverage begins on an anniversary of the closing date, one or more years after closing. The builder is responsible for structural repairs up to that date. If a covered problem occurs during the warranty period, the insurance company provides the repair.

Terms and conditions of these policies vary, and builders sometimes have a choice as to which coverage to provide. However, procedures for filing claims under any type of coverage are strictly enforced. Most impose a deductible or claim fee, and dispute resolution procedures are standard. If a home owner and a builder disagree over a warranty item, this procedure can resolve the issue usually faster and less expensively than legal action.

Warranty Claims

By now you may wonder how to decide whom to contact if something goes wrong. Your builder will tell you. Generally, two categories exist. Some builders ask that you report all items directly to them. Others provide a list of trade contractors who worked on the home. You contact the builder only if you did not receive a satisfactory response from a trade contractor. Most builders today fall into the former category. To monitor product quality, they must know about customer's complaints.

Emergency Service

Fortunately, emergencies do not occur often in new homes. When they do, most builders welcome a report by phone. Builders typically define emergencies as—

- total loss of heat
- in some climates, total loss of air-conditioning (This decision depends on local custom.)

- total loss of electricity
- a plumbing leak that requires you to shut off the entire water supply
- total loss of water
- gas leak (If the problem is inside the home, leave. Contact your utility company immediately and then notify the builder.)

Some builders arrange to have qualified staff members rotate on-call responsibilities. Others provide home owners with the emergency phone numbers of trade contractors for critical services: plumbing, electricity, and heating and air-conditioning. In an after-hours or weekend emergency, call the appropriate trade contractor or the builder's emergency number, according to your builder's instructions. Home owners usually think a roof leak is an emergency. Philosophically, the builder would agree. However, these repairs require a dry roof. The repairmen correct what they believe to be the problem, and everyone waits for a rain to test it. The leak sometimes reappears after several storms and causing frustration for everyone. After severe storms, notify your home owner's insurance company if you suspect any damage to the roof—one sure sign is seeing pieces of shingles in your yard.

No matter whom you call in an emergency, follow up in writing to your builder. If problems arise later, the first thing you need is documentation of what you reported and when. Your memory of a phone conversation may prove insufficient. If completing repairs after the emergency involves other trades, such as drywall and paint work after a plumbing leak, your written notification assures these items get into the system. Although emergency repairs are provided promptly, follow-up work goes through the nonemergency system and takes longer.

Nonemergency Service

Some builders suggest you report warranty items as you notice them. Others ask that you keep a list and submit claims at one or more checkpoints. Builders who follow this procedure typically schedule the first checkpoint for 30 to 90 days after move-in. These companies may send you a reminder that your warranty is about to expire near the end of the warranty period. However, remembering the expiration date of your warranty coverage is your responsibility.

Your builder is under no obligation to remind you of the pending expiration of your warranty period.

The checkpoint procedure is intended to produce more efficient service for all home owners. Everyone benefits when the builder can organize service activities according to a predictable schedule and produce a faster response time. However, this approach is not intended to deny you service. Between the builder's suggested checkpoints, if an item annoys you, send a request for repair.

One-Time Repairs. Many builders provide one-time repair of specific items. These might include repairs for shrinkage cracks or nail pops in drywall, caulking and grout, or settled spots in backfill areas. Review the specifics of what your builder offers in the written warranty standards. If your builder provides one-time repairs, you benefit by waiting until close to the end of the materials and workmanship warranty period to request them.

Put It in Writing. No matter what procedures the builder outlines for warranty service, put your service request in writing, sign and date it, and keep a copy in your house file. This procedure protects you by documenting what you reported and when. Processing also proceeds more accurately and completely. Your file contains a history of any recurring item, a paper trail that may enable your builder to obtain repairs from a manufacturer if a problem persists beyond the warranty. Finally, you may find having complete records of all work on your home useful when you sell your home.

Service Request Forms. Many builders provide printed forms like the one shown in Figure 14.3. These forms are convenient and standardize information for faster processing by the builder. Keep one accessible, perhaps on the side of the refrigerator. Jot down items you believe qualify for warranty repair. At the appropriate time, forward the list to your builder. If your builder does not provide these forms or if you do not have one, send a letter that includes the information shown in the sample in Figure 14.3.

Warranty Item Processing. Most warranty items are not emergencies. Upon receiving a warranty letter, the builder may schedule an inspection appointment with you to decide who should provide the repair. Your builder provides warranty action directly, through an employee, or indirectly, through a trade contractor. The builder informs the employee or trade contractor of the needed work, often via a written work order. You can see an example in Figure 14.4. Some builders forward a copy of these work orders to the home owner though this practice is not universal.

Response Time. The response time for new home warranty repairs can range from the same day to several weeks. Builders understand that home owners expect prompt service, but servicing homes is a unique challenge. You cannot drop off this product or ship it to the factory. Repairs may require the attention of one or more of several dozen trades. When you notify the builder of an item, you set off a chain of events:

- The builder screens the items.
- The builder notifies the appropriate trade contractor.
- The trade contractor notifies the fieldperson who performs repairs.
- Either the builder or the trade contractor orders material or parts.
- When the parts arrive, either the builder or the fieldperson arranges access to your home.

As with correcting orientation items, fewer and fewer builders accept keys. They prefer to have an adult present for repair work. Service work typically occurs Monday through Friday, between 7 a.m. and 4 p.m. Saturday appointments are sometimes available, but they are limited. Trade contractors seldom operate on weekends and most of the builder's staff is off as well. Builder employees who work Saturdays do not have the benefit of the complete support system. Your builder should list service hours in material you receive with your limited warranty.

If your builder does not accept keys or if you are uncomfortable providing one, either the builder or the designated serviceperson must contact you to set an appointment. Some builders set the appointments for trades to work in your home, although that can make communication more complicated. Others ask you to designate a date one to two weeks away and schedule all needed personnel for that day. Home owners' and builders' reactions to this approach have been favorable. However appointments are arranged, you do have an obligation to allow access to your home during normal business hours. You are under no obligation to allow anyone into your home without an appointment.

If either party misses the appointment, the process starts again. This cumbersome system results from the nature of the product: small, independent trade contractors do most of the work. Warranty work is usually completed within 5 to 30 business days, assuming you are available to allow access to the home. Sometimes work orders are put on hold until

Figure 14.3 Warranty Service Request

Please use this form to notify us of warranty items. Mail it to the address shown above. We will contact you to set an inspection appointment. Service appointments are available from 7 a.m. to 4 p.m., Monday through Friday. Thank you for your cooperation.

Name _____ Date _____

Street Address _____ City, State, Zip _____

Phone (Home)_____ Community _____

(Ms. Work) _____ Lot No. _____

(Mr. Work)_____ Plan _____

Email_____ Closing Date_____

Service Requested	**Service Action**
_____	_____
_____	_____
_____	_____
_____	_____
_____	_____

Comments _____

_____

_____

_____

_____

Home Owner_____ Date _____

Figure 14.4 Warranty Work Order

Date _____   Community _____

Work Order No. _____   Lot No. _____

Payment Approved _____   Model _____

Trade Contractor _____   Home Owner _____

Street Address _____   Street Address _____

City, State, Zip _____   City, State, Zip _____

Email _____   Email _____

Phone _____   Phone (Home) _____

Cell Phone _____   (Ms. Work) _____

                                        (Mr. Work) _____

Work Required _____

_____

_____

_____

                                        Requested by _____

Comments on Work Performed _____

_____

_____

                                        Completed by _____

                                        Date _____

The home owner has received a copy of this service order and will expect completion of this work within 10 business days. It is your responsibility to set a service appointment, although the home owner may call you to expedite this. Upon completion of the work, sign and return this form for the warranty file. Your attention and cooperation are appreciated.

you can conveniently schedule an appointment. This option works only when a delay does not increase the damage.

Kitchen Appliance Warranties

Appliance warranties are among the consumer products warranties your builder assigns or passes through to you (Figure 14.5). They generally last for one year, but some manufacturers cover specific parts for longer periods. This coverage usually provides only parts and you pay labor. Activate manufacturer warranties by completing and mailing any registration cards that come with the appliances. Follow recommended maintenance guidelines contained in these materials. Failure to do so can void your warranty.

Appliance manufacturers work directly with you if repairs are needed. You find service numbers in their use and care booklets. If you need to contact an appliance manufacturer, prepare to supply the model and serial number located on a sticker or metal plate attached to the appliance. The garbage disposal sticker is on the back or bottom of the unit. The easiest way to read it is to lie on the kitchen floor and stick your head in the cupboard.

Structural Repairs

Fortunately, few home owners file structural warranty claims. Structural repairs are often costly, time-consuming, and emotionally trying. Signs of structural movement or failure

Figure 14.5 Kitchen Appliances Usually Carry a Manufacturer's Warranty

Photo by James F. Wilson, Dallas, Texas.

of the load-bearing portions of a home usually appear in a pattern. Damage might involve cracks in the foundation, uneven floors, cracks in drywall, or ill-fitting doors and windows. Individually, each of these needed repairs can have an innocent explanation; in combination, they require inspection. Their exact cause can prove elusive.

The engineer who designed the foundation and structural system, the builder who installed it, and the home owner who owns it can each do everything right. Then Mother Nature gets the last word. And although many checks and balances exist to make certain each part of the home is sound, errors can occur. Either way, the builder or the warranty insurance company is primarily responsible. However, if a home owner's failure to maintain drainage has caused the problem, the home owner is responsible for repairs. If you believe your home shows signs of structural damage, notify your builder in writing. As important as written records are for minor items, they are vital when a structural warranty claim exists.

Detecting the cause of structural damage often requires a trained eye. Your builder may arrange for an inspection by a licensed professional engineer and request a written report. These reports contain several boilerplate paragraphs describing typical behavior of structural elements. The engineer draws on this knowledge and experience to deduce from surface evidence what is happening underground or inside walls.

The builder may need to remove a section of basement floor or expose another portion of the home's structural system to gain more insight. Often several visits occur to discern a pattern of movement. Once everyone believes the cause is determined, the builder can arrange corrective measures. After corrections are complete, the builder waits for confirmation that the home is stable before making cosmetic repairs. This wait can prevent the frustration of doing them twice. This inspect, wait, inspect, repair, wait, repair process can span several months and easily exceed the limits of human patience.

Disappointment and Disagreement

Warranties describe the boundary between the obligations of the builder, the trade contractors, the manufacturers, and the home owner. Most of the time, the separation of responsibility is clear: if you drive your car through the back of the garage, you should repair the damage to the wall (and the car). If the chimney falls off, the builder corrects that problem.

Gray Areas

Although warranty and maintenance are neither synonymous nor interchangeable, the boundary between the two can get fuzzy. The technical term for this fuzziness is "gray area." Too many possibilities exist to have a written standard for everything. Some items are subjective and setting a measurable standard for them is difficult, perhaps impossible. Consider these examples:

■ Builders usually warrant against drainline clogs for 30 days.

But what if you move in, leave town for 29 days, and return to find a clogged line?

■ A moving box staple may have caused the scratch you notice on the kitchen counter two days later, or maybe it was there before closing and no one noticed.

▪ When stained, wood shows color and pattern variation. The builder thinks the variation on your cabinets is normal. You believe strongly that it is too noticeable.

Interpretation of Standards

Builders temper a literal interpretation of warranty standards with common sense and often exceed those standards. Yet builders do deny service on items not covered by the limited warranty, or when the warranty has expired. What you can technically expect is what is in writing. To avoid unwelcome surprises, study the builder's limited warranty, warranty standards, and your maintenance responsibilities carefully when you sign the contract to build.

Review the builder's limited warranty, warranty standards, and your maintenance responsibilities again before moving into your home.

Some disagreements are not about warranty items at all, but they may take on the appearance of warranty issues. If you report a complaint to the builder after move-in, that report goes through the warranty system. One example is selector's remorse: one or more choices look different from what you expected, such as the hot pink countertop in the hall bathroom. This remorse does not mean the wrong color was installed (although that is possible).

Dye lots vary. Memories can fool the most astute customer. Seeing the full-size item is a surprise after selecting from a sample. You ask the builder to replace it. The builder checks to confirm that the item you selected was installed. If so, the claim does not qualify under the terms of the warranty: neither the material nor the workmanship is defective. The builder may offer to get you a price on the work or suggest a company with which you could work directly to arrange a replacement.

Another example is a detail you did not notice earlier that does not meet your approval, such as the underside of the snack bar being left unpainted. You ask the builder to paint it. The builder responds that your home is like the model, or per the specifications. Many buyers create a list of "shoulds" for their builder: a home of this price should include . . . should have . . . should be. . . . Again, you see the value of detailed plans and specifications. To assure your satisfaction make sure to negotiate and settle on what should come with your home. Reduce the conclusions to writing before you sign the contract.

Recourse

What do you do if you disagree with a warranty decision or feel dissatisfied with service work? Let your builder know in writing. Include a brief and objective history of the situation, mentioning information the builder may not know. Avoid editorializing, insulting, and threatening. Stick to dates, times, physical conditions, and documented commitments. End with a request that the builder visit your home to view the item and discuss alternatives.

Licensing Boards. In regions where a licensing board oversees builders, an appeal to that agency can resolve your complaint. Again, the procedure involves notice, inspections, and resolution. Licensing boards base their decisions on the established standards for the industry in that region. These standards may vary from another part of the country and from your personal standards. For more information, look in the government pages of your local directory for a number to call.

Warranty Insurance Claims. If your home included warranty insurance, file a claim with the insurance company. Include copies of previous correspondence to the builder. You'll find claim forms and other information in the policy documents. Processing by the insurance company may include an inspection of the home.

Alternative Dispute Resolution. If a solution still alludes you, follow the alternative dispute procedures outlined in the new home warranty. Remember this approach may be available to you with or without an insurance-backed warranty. Many builder warranties include a clause outlining an agreement on how to disagree. See Figure 14.6 for an example of an alternative dispute resolution clause. Finally, you can always just ask the builder to agree to an independent third party settling your dispute. If the builder agrees, a solution may result.

Small Claims Court. Note that most courts require you to use alternative dispute resolution if that requirement is included in your documents. If not, small claims court may be a possible option in your area. Filing a claim through small claims court does not require an attorney and is inexpensive. However, the size of the claim is limited by the local jurisdiction. On the date of your appearance you present your side, the builder presents the company's side, and the referee hands down a decision. For details and forms, contact your county court's small claims division.

Legal Action. Larger claims may require stronger legal action. Again, if dispute resolution is provided for, that recourse is usually the first action taken. The court's position is that with overflowing dockets, if an alternative to adding another case exists, the parties must try it. Some states make these procedures binding on both parties. In that case, the result represents your last opportunity for a solution. Legal battles are expensive, time-consuming, and quite upsetting. Both parties should make every effort to resolve their differences without litigation.

Figure 14.6 Alternative Dispute Resolution—Sample Language

Any and all disputes between the Builder and Owner arising out of the construction or sale of the described residential property, to include but not to be limited to matters of contract performance, negligence, express or implied warranties, and representations or disclosures, may initially be submitted to mediation before an impartial entity. Any mediated settlement shall be set out in written contract form and signed by the parties. Should any party decline to mediate, or should the mediation effort prove to be unsuccessful in resolving the matter, the parties agree to submit their dispute to binding arbitration in accordance with the construction industry rules of the American Arbitration Association. For disputes under $75,000, fast track rules shall be employed. All costs of mediation and arbitration shall be paid equally by each party, but such costs may be apportioned differently through mediated agreement or arbitration ruling.*

Owner_____ Builder _____

---

* Arbitration agreements should be prominently featured in the text of the contract or warranty agreement. Some jurisdictions require that to be enforceable the arbitration clause must be separately signed or initialed. Consult local counsel concerning the applicable law of the specific jurisdiction in regards to arbitration clauses.

Dramatic Tactics. Angry home owners sometimes want quicker revenge. Dramatic tactics such as picketing, front-yard signs, and the media may give you momentary gratification when you are angry. One frustrated home owner painted a sign on the back window of his mini-van. While the immediate gratification may feel good, over the long-term these tactics can hurt you more than the builder. If the community or your home develops a bad reputation at the same time it hurts the builder, the value of your home is affected.

A clear vision of the home you want and careful selection of a builder who can produce it prevents these problems. Stay involved in the planning and the building of that home, and perhaps most importantly, have realistic expectations about the results. Above all, take your time. Most conflicts between buyers and builders result from surprises that solid information and good communication prevent.

Few products combine science, technology, art, and sweat like a new home does. With informed expectations, you can enjoy the process and love the result. Your home is an investment. It is an expression of your personality, a source of pride, and a haven from the modern world. Few things compare to the satisfaction of turning the key in the door of your own home at the end of the day.

Glossary

A

affidavits or endorsements. These documents provide written confirmation that the property and buyers meet all requirements. One example is a *planned unit development* (PUD) endorsement that certifies that you have followed all home owners association covenants. Home buyers pay for the preparation and processing of such documents.

alternative dispute resolution. An agreement established at the start of the relationship regarding how disagreements will be resolved. This method avoids the cost and time of lawsuits and results may or may not be binding on the parties, depending on applicable state laws.

alternative materials. These items serve as replacements for wood in the construction of a house, for example, steel studs and foam core panels. Use of these materials can affect cost, the construction schedule, long-term performance as well as the home's impact on the environment.

appraisal fee. This fee covers the cost of appraising the property. Government-insured mortgages such as Veterans Administration (VA) or Federal Housing Administration (FHA) set the cost of the appraisal. The several-page resulting document may include photos of your home and those to which the appraiser compared it.

B

batter boards. A second set of stakes installed by the surveyor or the builder at a designated distance from the stakes that mark the outline of the home. The batter boards guide the excavator in digging the foundation.

builders, custom. They specialize in building one-of-a-kind homes starting with a blank computer screen or piece of paper. Custom builders tend to have small companies, both in volume (typically 10 or fewer a year) and number of employees. They may establish relationships with one or more architects or have one on staff. They organize their companies' systems and their personnel to build on isolated, scattered sites.

builders, design-build firms. The builder may be an architect or has an architect or designer on staff.

builder's limited warranty. Over 90 percent of builders provide a written limited warranty describing the terms and conditions under which repairs for covered defects are provided to the home owner. Most builders further provide written guidelines describing the standards used to define a defect and the typical repair that results.

builders, production. These builders organize their companies for high-volume construction. Local production builders might build as few as 20 homes a year; national firms as many as several thousand. Production builders offer a collection of floor plans, each with a choice of two or more exterior designs or elevations.

builders, semi-custom. They combine the characteristics of production and custom building. Their preexisting plans offer many possible variations. These builders typically are flexible about changes even if they require engineering and building department approval.

building envelope. The space available for building after subtracting *setbacks* and *easements.*

building permit. The document applied for by your builder and issued by the building department of your local jurisdiction that provides permission for your builder to build your home. It is based on other documents (such as a septic permit) required by the jurisdiction. The approval process usually includes a review of the plans and specifications submitted by the builder.

C

carbon monoxide. This odorless and colorless component of gases that are by-products of combustion in fireplaces, gas furnaces, water heaters, and clothes dryers causes headaches, nausea, fatigue, fainting, brain damage, and even death. Therefore you want to be sure these gases go out through a chimney or vent pipe. You can purchase an alarm designed to detect carbon monoxide for $30 to $60 at hardware stores. Follow instructions carefully for installation.

certificate of occupancy. After a review of the inspection records, survey, certifications, and other documents, the building department issues a certificate that permits the builder and the owners to close on the home (complete the sale). Without a certificate of occupancy you cannot close on the home nor move in.

change order. A form that authorizes your builder to make a change in your home. Making the change involved depends on your signing and paying for the change. Occasionally the builder will initiate a change order required because, for example, an appliance you chose is no longer available.

close of escrow. In some parts of the country an escrow agent handles closing, an escrow agreement specifies that the buyer and the seller each deposit required documents and funds with the escrow agent within a set time frame. The escrow agent records the necessary items, gives each party its share of the money and the papers. This type of closing takes place in steps. At some point you sign all the papers and deliver all the money. One or more days later, the escrow agent records the transaction. Once it is recorded, you own your home and can pick up your keys.

closing. Completing the sale of your home is called closing, settlement, or close of escrow. It is the process of transferring ownership of your home to you from the builder. It involves finalizing your mortgage loan, dispersing money to real estate agents, attorneys, a title company, surveyor, and probably others. It involves about 75 documents and nearly as many checks.

closing expenses. The charges due at closing. The Real Estate Settlement Procedures Act entitles you to see the charges on a standardized form (HUD-1 Settlement Statement) 24 hours before your closing appointment.

closing fee. The people who administered the paperwork receive this fee for their time and efforts.

CMU. This acronym stands for concrete masonry unit or a concrete block.

computer-aided design (CAD) systems. This software is used to design homes on the computer rather than a drawing board. The architect or designer can more easily and quickly change elements so you can see differences based on your choices, such as a different color for the kitchen cabinets or a fireplace added to the living room.

contingencies. Conditions imposed on the approval of a mortgage or other loan. You will need to supply written proof that you have met these conditions at closing.

copyright law. This law prohibits you and others from copying and using plans or changing them without permission of the copyright owner (the person who created them or a person who purchased the right to use them). That person could be an architect, designer, builder, or other person. You may need to purchase the plans for your house, pay a license fee to use them, or hire someone to create your own plans.

covenant protection. Restrictions that a home owners association places on the residents and homes in a community. A covenant may require design review of your house plans, architectural details, and exterior materials and colors. You may also need a design review of your landscaping plans.

credit report. An evaluation of your credit worthiness as assessed by one of three national credit-reporting companies. Giving permission for your lender to obtain a credit report is a routine part of a mortgage loan application.

critical path. This term refers to milestones in the building process that are critical to meeting the target delivery date.

D

deed. When your mortgage is paid off, this document conveys the home and lot to you, subject only to permitted exceptions such as a recorded easement.

developer. A company that prepares raw land for building, divides them into lots, and installs roads and utilities.

document preparation. You pay for the closing agent to assemble or prepare the documents you sign upon closing.

draw. Periodic payments to the builder from the lender or an escrow account per the draw schedule set up in the loan agreement.

driveway or street cut permit. Provides permission to install a driveway or cut a space in an existing curb for the driveway. If you or your builder needs a permit in your jurisdiction, you will need to pay a fee for the permit.

DSL lines. High-speed internet access lines.

E

easements. These spaces are set aside for the utility supply lines and other items to pass through the property. They allow service to your lot and those adjacent to it for now and the future. Many lots include drainage easements for the runoff from adjacent lots to cross your property. Easements are recorded and permanent.

express warranty. A warranty that is "expressed," usually in writing. Over 90 percent of home builders provide an express warranty that defines terms and conditions for provided repairs.

F

final number. The money you need to provide at closing. It includes prorated property tax and interest on your new loan—numbers that change daily.

finish materials. These items go over the sheathing. They could be siding, brick, stone, stucco, shingles, or a combination.

footprint. The space the house takes up on the ground.

form of payment. Depending on local practice you may need to bring cash or certified funds to closing.

G

"ghosting." Sooty stains on carpet and other surfaces of the home that results from incomplete combustion of hydrocarbons in scented candles and that are difficult and sometimes impossible to remove.

grading. Altering the slope of the lot is called grading. It is often done to drain water away from the house being constructed.

ground fault circuit interrupters (GFCI). These circuit breakers sense fluctuations in power and trip to prevent electrocution. Building codes require them for outlets in bathrooms, the kitchen, outside, and in the garage. You need to test them once a month.

H

hazard insurance premium. Your closing fees include one year's protection against loss by fire, wind, and other natural hazards. This coverage is usually part of the same home owner's policy that provides theft protection and liability protection in case your dog bites the mailman.

home owner orientation. The builder or his or her representative take the home buyer on a tour of the outside and the inside of the new home and demonstrate how to operate the various systems and appliances. This meeting provides an opportunity to ask any questions about operating and maintaining your new home.

HVAC. This acronym refers to the heating, ventilation, and air-conditioning systems in a home.

I

impact fee. A charge for the impact of your new home and its occupants on the infrastructure (roads, bridges, and the like) and community services (law enforcement, fire protection, schools, and others).

implied warranty. State statutes provide protection for consumers when they make purchases. The terms of the builder's written limited warranty, or its enforcement, may be impacted by such statutes.

improvement survey. A drawing the builder has the surveyor provide that shows the property boundaries, the home, the drive, and other improvements to the lot.

inspection card. A record of inspections performed by the building department. Sometimes this card and the building permit are combined into one document.

inspections. The building department will inspect your home for compliance with the applicable building code. Lenders, warranty insurance companies, the Federal Housing Administration (FHA), or Veterans Administration (VA) also may inspect your home. You also may hire a private inspector to check the house. Such inspectors focus on livability but would cite a code violation if they spot one.

insulation, batts. This insulation looks like thick narrow blankets and comes in various thicknesses. The insulation usually is made of fiberglass or cellulose although cotton is available, and variations are developing rapidly. Batts work best between studs.

insulation, blown. Small pieces of loose insulation that usually are applied through a large hose that blows them into hard to reach nooks in attics over the ceilings of the living spaces below. Wet spray cellulose can be mixed with a small amount of adhesive and sprayed on a framed wall. When it is dry any excess is scraped off the faces of the studs.

insurance-backed limited warranty. Insurance purchased by the home builder to protect the home owner against covered defects in the home in the event that the builder is unable or unwilling to repair them.

insurance, home owners. This insurance protects your home against fire, certain types of theft, and other items. You need to ask your insurance agent to list your lender as an insured (if the house is destroyed by fire your lender will be reimbursed). Be sure you provide the lender company's complete legal name. Closing requires a certificate of coverage showing the lender as an insured.

insurance, title. Such a policy would protect you in the event someone else claims to own your land.

J

junction box. These boxes protect the electric power supply connections from the grid to your home. Neither you nor your builder can control where the electric company places this box on your property. Small junction boxes protect the electrical connections between the walls of your home and between ceilings and the floors above them.

L

lender's inspection fee. The amount you pay at closing to cover the cost of inspection of your home by a lender's employee or an outside agency during construction, at each *draw,* and upon completion.

license, home builder's or contractor's. A document issued by many jurisdictions for a fee. It grants a builder the right to construct houses or other buildings within its boundaries.

loan discount or "points." Paying "points" up front reduces the interest rate on your loan. Each point equals 1 percent of the loan amount. Each point you pay reduces the interest rate about 1/8 of a percent.

lot, finished. A residential building site that is served by a street and utility lines is called a finished lot.

M

Magnuson-Moss Warranty Act. A federal law passed in 1975 to protect consumers by requiring certain details regarding consumer product warranty coverages to be disclosed to purchasers.

manufactured-wood products. Wood chips or veneers glued together to form stable materials of varying shapes and sizes for construction use.

manufacturer's warranty. This warranty protects the home owner against defects in the manufacturer's product. Typically during the home owner orientation, the builder's representative passes the manufacturer's warranty (along with use and care information) through to the home owner for such items as the stove, furnace, windows, and so on. The manufacturer's warranty may provide protection against defects in a product for a longer time period than the warranty coverage provided by the builder.

material and workmanship coverage. A common form of builder limited warranty coverage, material and workmanship warranties are typically for one year and provide for specified repairs if listed problems occur in your new home.

mechanical systems. These systems comprise the heating, ventilation, and air-conditioning (HVAC); plumbing; and electrical systems. They include the pipes, ducts, cables, and wires you do not see in a home and the fixtures, faucets, switches, and registers that you do see.

model homes. Production builders and semi-custom builders may have these sample houses already built that you can tour to get a clearer idea of what a particular floor plan would look like. Custom builders are not likely to build model homes because each home they build is unique. (However, some of them may agree to arrange an appointment with a former customer so you can see the quality of the company's construction.)

mortgage, adjustable rate. These loans have changeable interest rates and are typically easier to qualify for because of the lower initial payments.

mortgage, balloon. This loan for paying for a home requires small regular payments (sometimes just the interest amount) and a large payment when loan comes due.

mortgage or deed of trust. This document encumbers your home as security for repayment of the promissory note. Some states call this a mortgage, others a deed of trust. The result is the same: you must make your payments or risk losing your house.

mortgage, fixed rate. For this loan to pay for a house, the rate stays the same throughout the life of the loan—usually 15 or 30 years.

mortgage insurance application fee. If your down payment is less than 20 percent on a conventional loan you will have to buy mortgage insurance. This fee pays for the administration costs of processing your application for that insurance.

mortgage insurance premium. When your mortgage insurance is approved, you pay the first year's fee and several months of premium to establish a reserve at the closing.

Multiple Listing Service. A computer-based system which real estate professionals can join to have access to thousands of details about homes and properties that are available in the marketplace.

N

nail pops. Nails heads stick out from the surface into which they were originally pounded. A nail pop occurs when the wood that a nail is in shrinks and squeezes the nail out.

notary fee. You pay this fee to certify that you are the person signing the documents to close on your home.

O

Occupational Safety and Health Administration (OSHA). This U.S. Government office creates and enforces regulations relating to safety and health for residential construction.

orientation. See *home owner orientation.*

origination fee. This fee covers compensation for the loan officer and the lender's administration costs. It typically is 1 percent of your loan.

P

percolation test. Measures the rate at which soil absorbs water. This rating determines the size of the septic system that would be needed for a house on the lot. Some builders and others call it a perc test.

permit fee. The fee your builder pays for a permit to build, tap into a water or sewer line, or other privilege or permission.

plan check fee. Imposed by the building department, this fee is the cost of checking the details of your plans to be sure they meet the applicable building code.

planning board. This board comprises a group of citizens guided by community goals that oversees land use and the pace of development for its jurisdiction.

promissory note. This note from you is payable to the lender in the principal amount of the loan, plus interest. Sign only one copy, unless you are willing to pay for your home more than once. You will sign and receive riders describing interest rate adjustments if you have that type of loan.

premium. You would pay this additional fee to garner a corner lot or a better view.

R

radon. This invisible and odorless gas forms as a by-product of decaying uranium in the soil. Depending on local geology and weather, it can enter any house. Winter is the best time to test for its presence.

resale home. This euphemism means a previously owned home.

roll crush. This phenomenon results from rolling and storing carpet. The part of the carpet on the bottom gets squished by the weight of the carpet in the roll. It takes longer to fluff up when the carpet is unrolled.

S

selections. The items that you need to choose promptly so materials and parts can be delivered in time to meet the schedule for constructing your home. Custom-made items (such as hand-painted tiles) require longer lead times than standard items.

set backs. These required distances from the edges of the lot or any *easement* tell you the space in which you cannot build. They usually are not the same for each edge of the lot.

settlement agent. This person orchestrates the closing including ordering the title work and property survey and organizing the paperwork for the closing. Fees and services can vary so compare them and choose carefully.

sheathing. This material protects the interior of the house from wind and water from rain, melted snow, or condensation. The roofing and the exterior finish materials, such as siding, brick, stone, and the like, go over the sheathing.

site survey. A diagram that outlines the shape and measurements of a potential building site. Easements, set-backs, and other restrictions can impact the size and shape of the space where the home can be built.

site visits, random. Your builder may set guidelines for days and times when you can make visits not included in the schedule of meetings. The prime reasons for these guidelines are your safety, satisfaction, and the smooth flow of work.

site visits, scheduled. These visits give you and your builder an opportunity to have each other's undivided attention. At agree-upon points during construction you meet at the site to review progress, discuss questions, and update the target delivery date. These visits might occur every week or two or only upon completion of certain phases of work.

sound pollution. Noise.

special district fee. This fee helps to pay for the impact of your new house and your living in it on the roads, law enforcement, fire protection, schools, and other community services. It is similar to an *impact fee* or *use tax.*

specifications. A description of the construction of your house down to minor details and the items that will go into it such as a furnace and kitchen appliances.

stakes. Pieces of 1×2-inch wood that, with colored ties, the surveyors pound into the ground to mark the location of the home. The builder or the surveyor installs a second set of stakes (called batter boards) a designated distance from the first set. The excavator uses the second set of stakes as a guide to dig the foundation.

stick built method. When the framers build the roof with individual pieces of lumber that are sawed and nailed on the job, they are using the stick built method.

structural changes. These changes involve the load-bearing parts of your home.

structural coverage. That portion of a builder's limited warranty coverage that protects you against failure of load-bearing elements of your home.

systems coverage. Usually for a two-year period, this warranty coverage protects you from failure of plumbing, heating, and electrical lines that circulate services through your home. Note that fixtures (sinks, chandeliers, and so on) are covered only under the one-year material and workmanship coverage and are excluded from systems coverage. Not all builder warranties provide systems coverage, but it is typical in an insurance-backed warranty.

T

tap fees. The charges for tapping into the municipal water and sewer systems.

target date. This date is the initial goal for completion of your house. The final date of completion is subject to delays for weather, missing deliveries, illnesses, and other problems.

title. This document provides proof of ownership. You receive the title to your home when the mortgage is paid off or for any vehicle you purchase. The title is registered in the jurisdiction in which you live.

title search. This search confirms that the seller has the right to sell you the property you are buying and that no one else has any claim to it. The title insurance company bases its policy covering the title on this search.

title insurance commitment. The title insurance company will mail you the actual policy in the weeks following your closing. When you receive this commitment, keep the document in a safe place with your other important papers. The document you see at closing simply promises to issue the policy. Title insurance is required in the amount of the mortgage to protect the lender if the title search missed anything.

traffic. In addition to vehicle movement this term refers to movement of people in a home. Before purchasing a new home, you need to check the floor plan to see that the traffic patterns in the house match your lifestyle. The term also refers to people visiting sales offices, model homes, and home sites.

trusses. Hollow triangles or other shapes composed of wood or metal parts that provide support, usually for the roof of a house. They often are constructed in factories in a controlled environment and delivered to the site ready to lift into place. A boom truck may do the lifting as the crew attaches each truss in its correct location.

U

use tax. This tax helps pay for the impact of your new house and your living in it on the roads, law enforcement, fire protection, schools, and other community services. It is similar to an *impact fee* or *special district fee.*

References

Bower, John. *The Healthy* House. Bloomington, Ind.: The Healthy House Institute, 2001. Available at healthy@bloomington.in.us

Building Your New Home. Washington, D.C.: BuilderBooks.com, National Association of Home Builders, 2001. Available at www.builderbooks.com.

Buying Your Home: Settlement Costs and Information. Washington, D.C.: Office of Housing, Federal Housing Administration, U.S. Department of Housing and Urban Development. Available at http://www.hud.gov/offices/hsg/sfh/res/stcosts.pdf.

Buying Your New Home. Washington, D.C.: BuilderBooks.com, National Association of Home Builders, 2003. Available at www.builderbooks.com.

Consumer Handbook on Adjustable Rate Mortgages. Produced in cooperation with the National Association of Home Builders and 17 other organizations and agencies. Washington, D.C.: Office of Thrift Supervision, Federal Reserve Board. Available at www.federalreserve.gov/pubs/brochures/arms/arms.pdf (254K).

Crump, David. *Copyright Law for Home Builders.* Washington, D.C. BuilderBooks, National Association of Home Builders, 2004. Available at www.builderbooks.com; under the masthead, click on the words *Digital Delivery,* read the directions, then click on the word, *Legal.*

"Floor Plans, Carolina Dreamin'," "Layouts for Living" Section, *Nation's Building News Online,* June 6, 2005. http://www.nbnnews.com/NBN/issues/2005-06-06/Front+Page/2.html

Garton-Good, Julie. *All About Mortgages: Insider Tips to Finance or Refinance Your Home.* Chicago: Dearborne Trade Publishing, 2004.

Gerhart, James. *Caring for Your Home.* Washington, D.C.: BuilderBooks.com, National Association of Home Builders, 2003. Available at www.builderbooks.com.

Get the Facts on Mold (brochure). Washington, D.C.: BuilderBooks.com, National Association of Home Builders, 2002. Available at www.builderbooks.com.

Glink, Ilyce R. *100 Questions Every First Time Home Buyer Should Ask.* Three Rivers, Mich.: Three Rivers Press, due out 2005.

Home Mortgages: The Mortgage Application Process: Some Things to Expect. Washington, D.C.: Board of Governors, Federal Reserve System. Available at www.federalreserve.gov/pubs/mortgage/MORBRO_2.HTM.

Looking for the Best Mortgage: Shop, Compare, Negotiate. Washington, D.C.: Board of Governors, Federal Reserve System. Available at www.federalreserve.gov/pubs/mortgage/mortb_1.htm.

Petit, Jack, Debra L. Bassert, and Cheryl Kollin. *Building Greener Neighborhoods: Trees as Part of the Plan.* Washington, D.C.: American Forests and Home and BuilderBooks.com, National Association of Home Builders, 1995. Available at www.builderbooks.com; under the masthead, click on the words *Digital Delivery,* read the directions, then click on the words *Land Development.*

Smith, Carol, *Homeowner Manual: A Template for Home Builders,* 2nd ed. Washington, D.C.: BuilderBooks, 2001.

Your New Home and How to Take Care of It. Washington, D.C.: BuilderBooks.com, National Association of Home Builders, 2003. Available at www.builderbooks.com.

Index